# tune in

# ALSO BY SONIA CHOQUETTE

## Books/Oracle Cards

*The Answer Is Simple . . . Love Yourself, Live Your Spirit!*
*The Answer Is Simple Oracle Cards*
*Ask Your Guides: Connecting to Your Divine Support System*
*Ask Your Guides Oracle Cards*
*Diary of a Psychic: Shattering the Myths*
*The Fool's Wisdom Oracle Cards*
*Grace, Guidance, and Gifts: Sacred Blessings to Light Your Way*
*The Intuitive Spark: Bringing Intuition Home to Your Child, Your Family, and You*
*Soul Lessons and Soul Purpose: A Channeled Guide to Why You Are Here*
*Soul Lessons and Soul Purpose Oracle Cards*
*The Time Has Come . . . to Accept Your Intuitive Gifts!*
*Traveling at the Speed of Love*
*Trust Your Vibes at Work, and Let Them Work for You*
*Trust Your Vibes Oracle Cards*
*Trust Your Vibes: Secret Tools for Six-Sensory Living*
*Vitamins for the Soul: Daily Doses of Wisdom for Personal Empowerment*

## CD Programs

*Ask Your Guides: How to Connect with Your Spiritual Support System*
(6-CD and 4-CD sets)
*Attunement to Higher Vibrational Living,* with Mark Stanton Welch (4-CD set)
*Meditations for Receiving Divine Guidance, Support, and Healing* (2-CD set)
*The Power of Your Spirit: A Guide to Joyful Living* (6-CD set)
*Trust Your Vibes at Work, and Let Them Work for You* (4-CD set)
*Trust Your Vibes: Secret Tools for Six-Sensory Living* (6-CD set)

All of the above are available at your local
bookstore, or may be ordered by visiting:

Hay House USA: www.hayhouse.com®
Hay House Australia: www.hayhouse.com.au
Hay House UK: www.hayhouse.co.uk
Hay House South Africa: www.hayhouse.co.za
Hay House India: www.hayhouse.co.in

※

# tune in

## LET YOUR INTUITION GUIDE YOU TO
### Fulfillment and Flow

*Sonia Choquette*

**HAY HOUSE, INC.**
Carlsbad, California • New York City
London • Sydney • Johannesburg
Vancouver • Hong Kong • New Delhi

*Published and distributed in the United States by:* Hay House, Inc.: www.hay house.com® • *Published and distributed in Australia by:* Hay House Australia Pty. Ltd.: www.hayhouse.com.au • *Published and distributed in the United Kingdom by:* Hay House UK, Ltd.: www.hayhouse.co.uk • *Published and distributed in the Republic of South Africa by:* Hay House SA (Pty), Ltd.: www.hayhouse.co.za • *Distributed in Canada by:* Raincoast: www.raincoast.com • *Published in India by:* Hay House Publishers India: www.hayhouse.co.in

*Cover design:* Amy Rose Grigoriou • *Interior design:* Tricia Breidenthal

This is a revised and expanded edition of *The Power of Your Spirit* (ISBN: 978-1-4019-2810-0).

#### Library of Congress Cataloging-in-Publication Data

Choquette, Sonia.
Tune in : let your intuition guide you to fulfillment and flow / Sonia Choquette.
   pages cm
ISBN 978-1-4019-4310-3 (tradepaper : alk. paper) 1. Intuition. I. Title.
BF315.5.C56 2013
153.4'4--dc23

153.44

2013010967

**Tradepaper ISBN: 978-1-4019-4310-3**

16  15  14  13    4  3  2  1
1st edition, September 2013

Printed in the United States of America

SUSTAINABLE FORESTRY INITIATIVE
Certified Chain of Custody
Promoting Sustainable Forestry
www.sfiprogram.org
SFI-01268
SFI label applies to the text stock

To the Holy Spirit, the Divine Source of All Life.
I offer this book in humble service to, and in
deepest gratitude for, your never-ending loving
light upon us all. Thank you for the gift of my life.

# CONTENTS

# INTRODUCTION

"This above all: to thine own self be true."

— **William Shakespeare**

Several months ago, I found myself in a hotel room in San Diego after presenting an all-day workshop to several hundred people. Tired and ready to relax, I decided to order room service and rent a movie. After skimming through the selections for something light and funny, I finally settled on a romantic comedy called *My Life in Ruins*.

The movie itself was cute enough, but the main character's struggle actually made a big impression on me. Georgia, a young Greek-American tour guide living in Greece, is unhappy and frustrated. Her friends tell her it's because she has lost her *kefi*, a Greek word for inner voice, or "Spirit." To them, this is the obvious reason for her misery and why nothing in her life seems to work out. To make matters worse, no person or event can change her situation. It's up to Georgia to rediscover her magic power, her kefi. Otherwise, her world will remain colorless, uninspiring . . . and most likely, loveless. Only she can uncover her inner spark and get back into the flow of life.

Like most Hollywood stories, this one has a happy ending. Georgia relaxes her rigid mental control over things, opens up to her feelings, and lets herself connect with the wonderful world around her. By following her inner promptings, she finds that her life once again has profound meaning, laughter, and love. That night I went to sleep feeling happy and relieved. One more person who tuned back in to her intuition and followed her Spirit—even if only in the movies—meant one less miserable person in the world. Hurray!

The film reminded me that the problem and pain of tuning out your intuition, the voice of your Spirit, isn't that unusual. In fact, it might be the most common problem from which people suffer today. It's certainly the most common issue I've seen in my 35 years of experience as a professional intuitive counselor and teacher. Through my one-on-one intuitive sessions and the classes I teach, I work intimately with thousands of men and women all over the world each year. I continually encounter incredibly talented, creative, and caring individuals who feel lost, disillusioned, and powerless. Yet most of them also know in their hearts that there is another way to live. If only they would tune in and listen to what their intuition, their Spirit, is telling them, things might be very different.

### Tuning In to Your Inner Voice

We all want to successfully deal with life's challenges, face disappointment with grace, express ourselves creatively, and feel excited by a meaningful purpose. We want to be more spontaneous and carefree—laughing or singing out loud and dancing with abandon. We want to open our hearts, leave our fears behind, and find genuine peace no matter what is happening around us. To put it simply, like Georgia, we want to reclaim our kefi and let our intuition lead the way.

But first we must realize that our ego self, the self that we have constructed in order to interact with the outside world, cannot take us to this kind of inner freedom and exuberance. In fact, it cannot lead us at all to the things we most desire in life. For these profound, transformational experiences we must learn to reach more deeply into ourselves, beneath our outer ego shielding—not in an attempt to transcend or get over the ego, but rather as a means to connect more directly to our inner selves, wherein our Spirit dwells.

We all have a Spirit-given inner joy and exuberance for life, even if we're not in touch with it at the moment. There are any number of understandable reasons why we may lose touch with this joy, such as growing up in difficult family circumstances where life was harsh and it felt unsafe to trust anyone or anything, let alone our Spirit. Many of us may have been in touch with our joy earlier in life, but broken relationships, challenging financial circumstances, illness, or even the loss or death of a loved one may have left us feeling depressed and uncertain. In either case, it's important to realize that it *is* possible to return to joy, to find and follow Spirit once again.

But as much as we wish for such liberation, as much as we long to feel and express our Spirit-given sense of inner joy, longing alone isn't enough. We want the gifts of our intuition to flow, but unless we engage in the practical steps necessary to make that happen—unless we reach beyond the superficial managing of our ego selves—we remain stuck and more discouraged than ever. Taking the first step can be hard; life circumstances can seem so overwhelming that we feel as if we don't have the time or energy to make changes right now. We may resist for fear that focusing on ourselves is self-indulgent—just the thought of it leaves us feeling too stressed and guilty to make a change. When it comes to living an authentically guided and satisfying life, we're like window-shoppers on Madison Avenue, gazing longingly at the incredible possibilities dangling before our eyes, yet not stepping in and claiming them as our own. We're afraid that the cost of the effort is too high, not just in monetary terms, but also in the cost of asking for support and taking the time and allocating the energy needed to do something new and exciting for ourselves.

Given the thousands of conversations I've had with clients about this over the years, I've observed that even if we overcome our fear of change, we can still run into problems accessing our inner Spirit and the guidance it provides us through intuition. Far too many of us are stuck in our heads, trying to think our way back to our true selves, when the only real path to our inner Spirit is through our hearts. Intuition is not something we *think*. It's something we *feel* in our heart, where our Spirit dwells. Once we tune in to what we feel in our heart and Spirit, our intuition kicks into gear and starts to communicate with us in so many delightful ways. While becoming aware of our intuition, our guiding Spirit, is a great start toward creating a better life, it is just that—a start. *Knowing* what we are intuitively guided to do will make no difference in our lives whatsoever unless we actually choose to follow through and *act* on our intuition in a timely way. Oftentimes, the thought of fearlessly following our inner guidance simply scares us, so we remain frozen, feeling the call to live differently, but not heeding it.

The encouraging truth is that we don't have to leap into the void of blind faith when it comes to trusting our intuition and following our inner guidance over our fears, as some people believe is necessary. That's one way (a good way, in fact, as I can personally attest, as evidenced by the time I abruptly left college and moved to France only to be met with all sorts of magical experiences that I'll share with you later in the book), but happily, not the *only* way to get into the flow of our true Self. There is a more gradual alternative. We can gently become aware of and follow our intuition, step-by-nonthreatening-step, by paying attention to our inner promptings, by simply being more aware of and honest about the choices we make, and by noticing what feels right in our heart and what doesn't. What will ease and support this shift is adopting a few simple daily practices that will help to focus our attention inward and acknowledge our intuition, and then take the *baby steps* needed in order to follow through to action.

For example, I have a client named Anita who, as a scientist, found it very difficult to successfully tune in to and trust her intuition, as her rigorous intellectual training made her skeptical of things beyond the boundaries of the physical realm. She had never been able to form any long-lasting, intimate relationships with a man and now, at 43 years old, she was distressed enough about this sad state of emotional affairs to ask me for some help. I shared with her several simple tools, which I'll introduce to you later in this book, one of which was simply to breathe more deeply and pay closer attention to the world around her. Admitting that she was preoccupied much of the time, she took my advice, acknowledging that it made sound scientific sense to do so. Within weeks she noticed that she had become much more relaxed and present by practicing this simple tool of awareness, and she began to be more open and at ease with others.

One day Anita had the spontaneous intuitive hit to invite her neighbor—a woman who lived in the same condo and whom she bumped into nearly every day in the elevator—over for dinner. She readily accepted Anita's invitation and, at the last minute, called to ask if she could bring along her older brother, who had just moved to town following a messy divorce. Long story short, Anita and her neighbor's brother found they had a lot in common and began a friendship of their own, which in time led to something deeper, and now they're engaged. Anita is still surprised by how these events unfolded—how simply learning to breathe helped her tune in to and follow her intuition to reach out, leading to her present and surprising relationship—all over a matter of a few short months. That is how intuition works! It begins with simple shifts in awareness, followed by simple shifts in action, leading to gloriously positive shifts in experience.

Acting on our intuition is one of the most empowering choices we can make in our lives. We can't control the outside world, but by tuning in, listening to our Spirit, and following our intuition, we *can* begin to chart a new course—one that brings about deep satisfaction and personal peace—regardless of what's going on around us. Navigating through life, we are like a boat at sea. Intuition is the rudder that helps us to maintain our true course when wind and weather try to push us off of it.

When we lose touch with our intuition, or find ourselves too distracted or insecure to trust what we feel inside, we fall out of integrity with our true Self and surrender our creative ability to respond to life's circumstances, leaving us with limited ways of finding authentic peace and well-being. All too often we've been conditioned by generally well-intentioned people, such as our parents, teachers, or bosses—those who have had our best interests in mind, for the most part—to follow others' or society's rules over our own intuition. Chronically doing so, however, only leads us further and further away from our center, our creativity, our Spirit.

No matter how we got there, as long as we continue to tune out our intuition, we will continue to feel out of sorts, off our game, lost, frustrated, and even like an imposter in our own lives. The perpetual stress and internal chaos of ignoring intuition can even cause physical and psychological harm. The more I study people, the more I'm convinced that continually disregarding intuition is the root cause for most depression, distraction, addiction, disease, and discontent. But the worst consequence of living a life tuned out to our guiding Spirit is that we lose touch with the ability to feel as though we're making a meaningful contribution, which is what gives our lives a sense of purpose.

### Shift in Consciousness

Thankfully, these days more and more people are committed to living a spiritually empowered, authentically grounded, intuitively guided, positive, and peaceful life. We're generally becoming much more willing to accept the idea that we are spiritual beings who create our own reality and aren't simply victims of circumstance, as evidenced by a huge surge of interest in such things as quantum physics and mind-body medicine. We're more willing to explore and discuss our rich inner lives and our ever-expanding intuitive experiences. And yet, in spite of these encouraging signs, we're still suffering with, and causing some of, the worst personal and worldwide violence and earthly destruction that humankind has ever known.

Incidents of suicide and drug addiction have spiraled out of control, for example. The environment is under siege. Our relationships with each other (and among nations) are blasting apart, sometimes tragically with guns and other weapons. So even though the *idea* of spiritual awakening and personal empowerment sounds appealing and even possible, the actual shift in consciousness most of us need to make in order to go from victim of circumstance to Divine co-creator has yet to occur for most of us. We all must take a big step forward—if not an actual leap—to jump-start the transformation that everyone speaks of and desires . . . and the world so desperately needs. Our inner peace contributes to the world's peace.

A life where we believe that we aren't making a meaningful contribution feels like a life wasted. People in this state tend to find negative ways to distract themselves and deaden the emptiness they experience. Whether this leads to destructive behaviors or emotions, frequent accidents or illnesses, career stalls or chronic unemployment, or outbursts of rage or social withdrawal, soon the problem becomes other peoples' problem as well. All paths are interwoven—we are connected to one another, and one person's misery eventually affects everyone else. Therefore, not only is tuning in to our inner guidance an essential personal need, it's also a profoundly important familial and social need.

Listening to the voice of your intuition—instead of the voice of your fears and other peoples' wishes and instructions—will bring about, over time, a deep-seated, unwavering sense of profound integrity, creative inspiration, and grounded soul purpose. Tuning in to and following your intuition relaxes your mind, puts your body at ease, and opens your heart because you eliminate inner conflict as you become more at one with your Spirit, your true Self. Following your Spirit brings about an inner sense of peace, eliminates distraction, and helps you be more open. With such a big load off your shoulders, you can begin to fine-tune your awareness and expand your creativity, gaining a more graceful, fulfilling, and productive rhythm in your life. With your Spirit firmly at the helm, you flow with the deepest, most authentic truth of your being and experience each day as God designed and intended you to experience it: perfect, beautiful, connected, and filled with joy. Because you're aligned with your true Self, you feel less and less compelled to seek approval or self-worth in how others view you. You stop feeling out of sync with yourself, and that's a huge relief.

In following your intuition and trusting your Spirit, not only do you feel uplifted, but you also uplift everyone you come in contact with. Because we are sentient beings and are affected by one another's energy, others will sense your genuine ease and consequently relax more in your company. Many of the typical challenges you might expect, such as experiencing others as overly cautious or suspicious, will seem to suddenly ease, replaced with more heart-to-heart, creative, trusting, and positive connections.

Guided by your intuition, your Spirit opens your eyes to fresh perspectives, reveals new opportunities, and showers you with synchronistic moments that bring a sense of certain magic into your life. Even those who have been habitually difficult to deal with, such as set-in-their-ways family members or hardened bosses, won't trouble you as much, as your intuition also often brings with it more objectivity, deeper insight, and better understanding of people. You become more compassionate, recognizing others' negative behavior as a symptom of having lost touch with their inner voice, their Spirit, so it's easier not to take their unpleasant or obnoxious behavior personally. In fact, often those who are not in the habit of being easygoing will change their behavior when in your company because your personal vibration is generally so positive they can't help but start to entrain with it. With your Spirit guiding, you will feel lighter and clearer, and your world will brighten up. You will start to really love yourself and your life, and that's the best reward of all.

Honoring our inner voice and allowing our Spirit to lead is the inevitable choice we must all eventually make if we hope to live together in peace. Choosing otherwise keeps us battling our own fears and battling others. This choice hurts us, each other, and our planet. Those who refuse for whatever reason to surrender to their intuition, their heart, and their Spirit will continue to suffer, to struggle, and to miss out on the joys of life. Like a battery running out of power, unless we stop fighting and start trusting our Spirit for guidance, our limited ego energy will dwindle and die.

I feel confident that sooner rather than later we will all come to realize the limitations of the ego, and accept the power that lies within our Spirit because that is the purpose of our soul's journey on Earth.

Reaching for this book on a shelf or having it fall into your hands in some other way is a strong indication that, on a deep level, you're ready to start living in greater alignment with your authentic Self. Maybe this is your first step toward that end. Maybe you've already taken steps along the path toward living your life this way. No matter what got you to this page, deciding to allow your intuition to lead the way will soon have you leaving fear behind and enjoying the bounty and joy that come with living in the flow.

### The Road Ahead

Making the decision to follow your intuition and live your Spirit is relatively straightforward; carrying it out isn't always easy to do, however. As you shift back to honoring your authentic Self, you can realistically expect to be challenged again and again to face your fears and stand up for your truths. Although tuning in to your intuition and tuning out the pressures of the outside world can at times be difficult, it brings about such a positive transformational experience that with a little effort you will never go back to the old way of letting patterns of fear be your guide.

The process of tuning in to your intuition and living your Spirit generally unfolds in four distinct steps, each one propelling you to the next. How fast or slow you move through them depends on your present level of discomfort, your intention to shift, your desire to find more satisfaction and inner peace, the courage to stand up for your new choices, and last, but most important, practice. Once you commit to honoring your intuition, get ready! You're about to embark on the most exciting, joyous ride of your life; and I promise that you'll love it.

Tuning in to your intuition isn't as big a deal as it might seem because it is, after all, the way you were naturally designed to live. It begins with paying attention to your daily choices; unlearning and undoing bad, dead-end habits; and changing inaccurate beliefs about yourself that haven't served you very well, such as believing you aren't worthy of love and happiness or capable of making good choices for yourself. It also means developing the habit, or establishing the ritual, of tuning in to your Spirit every day: listening inward, trusting what you feel, letting go of the fearful need to control things, opening your heart, building the courage to take charge of your life, and following through on your intuition until it becomes second nature—and ultimately, the only way you choose to live.

The transformation will not be immediate; rather, you'll learn to do these things step-by-step, much like learning to dance. At first it may all seem overwhelming or too much to think about, so *not* like you, but with a little practice, I assure you that this new way of doing things will start falling into place. Sooner than you can ever imagine, it will be as if you've been dancing with Spirit forever, and you won't be able to imagine living any other way.

❊ ❊ ❊

# Chapter One

# STEPPING UP:
# HOW TO USE THIS BOOK

After more than 35 years of experience teaching people how to tune in to their intuition and follow their Spirit, I've learned there are four distinct steps you must pass through to become free of your fears and get back into flow with your authentic Self: *Waking Up, Digging Deep, Taking the Leap,* and *Entering the Flow.* As you take each step of returning to Spirit, you move further away from the trance and traps of fearful, limiting, false perceptions, and closer to your true nature and real joy. Although it's possible to move through all four steps in one dramatic swoop (and I've seen this happen), I have found this to be a rare exception.

Most people generally approach following their intuition cautiously, gaining confidence as they go, depending on their results. That only works up to a point, however. Eventually you have to throw caution to the wind and learn to "live life true" instead, following your intuition and inner truth no matter how unsafe it may initially feel.

There are times, especially early on, when following your intuition may cause you or others anxiety because you're thwarting a lifetime of conditioning to the contrary. For example, what did people tell you when you left college and decided to travel for a year before getting a job or starting a career? What did people say when you decided to quit your career in law and go to beauty school or become a massage therapist instead? Can you recall times when you might have changed course or moved in a new direction because you heard a call from within to do something different, unexpected, or untested, and yet you weren't sure it was the right thing to do? Do you remember how you felt at times like these? This kind of anxiety is what we all experience when moving away from the familiar, known, or predetermined course of action. Consider this anxiousness as a positive growing pain, and one you can manage with deep breathing, focus, and the determination to be true to yourself. You'll find that this kind of anxiety quickly turns into excitement and adventure once you begin to follow your intuition over both your inner objections and fears and those of others.

This is very different from the kind of anxiety you experience when you *don't* follow your intuition. It feels inwardly very dissonant, even subtly alarming, as though you've drifted off course, and no matter how hard you try to ignore it, you remain filled with stress. You simply don't feel like you're being true to yourself, no matter how well you perform or things appear on the outside. Like wearing a shoe that doesn't fit, the discomfort that comes from not listening to your intuition is a warning signal that your outward lifestyle does not match your inner Spirit. Only by changing course and aligning with your deep inner voice will this anxiety begin to lift. Happily, both kinds of anxiety are resolved with the same remedy, which is to follow your intuition. Once you do, anxiety shifts into renewed energy and a sense of personal, unshakable power.

Ultimately, your motivation—and hence the pace of your return to Spirit—will be based on how badly things are working out for you the old, "safe" way; how uncomfortable you are with the status quo; how necessary you feel it is to change; and how moved you feel to live in a more honest and authentic way. You are in control. In my experience, most people accelerate their pace rather quickly. Once you take the leap, you'll begin to enjoy the deeply rewarding positive experiences you'll have each time you choose to tune in to your Spirit and follow your intuition. You will be flowing.

### A Step at a Time

I've set up the book to help you recognize each step, learn all you can when in it, and still keep moving until you're at the center of your heart and Spirit and tuned in to your intuition for good. Consider each of the four steps as being like real steps, with landings between them. These landings, or plateaus, enable you to rest, re-equilibrate, and absorb the lessons of the last step before ascending to the next one. Unless you're a spiritual athlete, pushing straight up the steps may leave you dizzy and out of breath—better to take the steps one at a time and attain the summit centered and whole.

I illustrate each of the four steps with stories from both my practice and my own life. Each story is then accompanied by three follow-up sections: "Tuning In," which further explores the lesson the story teaches; "Asking the Questions," a series of questions designed to help you reflect on where these lessons apply to your life; and "Daily Ritual," a simple daily practice to help you anchor and strengthen your ability to tune in to your Spirit and follow your intuition in the most natural and easy way. These activities will help you to solidify and internalize each step's wisdom.

In the middle of the book, after Step One, *Waking Up*, where you begin to notice you're off course and start to become aware of your inner voice, and Step Two, *Digging Deep*, where you begin to search for evidence that following your intuition is a sound and right choice for you, I pause for a moment and introduce you to the concept and ritual of setting up a personal altar in your home or private space, as an aid to establishing the regular practice of tuning in to your Spirit, God, Universal Good, and all of your heavenly helpers for daily guidance and support. In most parts of the world outside of the West, people have altars in their homes and use them as places in which to meditate, focus, pray, send out requests for help, and above all, to express gratitude for all the guidance and help that they receive from their Spirit each and every day.

Having an active altar (and by *active* I mean a place where you actively go to do all of the above) offers a soul-enriching, wonderful, grounding opening into the Spirit world. The minute I stand or sit before my own altar, I am quickly led to an inner place of peace and harmony. In addition to being a beautiful thing to behold, an altar serves as an "on" switch to your deeper Spirit and inner truth and acts as a portal leading you to the subtle realms of Spirit. The more regularly you practice the ritual of sitting or standing in front of your altar, the more quickly your mind will learn to switch over and tune in to your Spirit, much like when you step into a temple, mosque, or church. The more frequently you visit your altar, the higher spiritual vibration it will hold, energetically pulling you inward to that sacred place. Creating an altar opens a lost gateway for so many people and fills a void you may not even know exists. I hope you enjoy this section of the book and are intrigued enough to create an altar of your own for these higher healing purposes.

I follow this interlude by resuming our journey and walking you through the last two steps—*Taking the Leap* and *Entering the Flow*—complete with more stories to illustrate these steps, followed by questions to address and simple practices and rituals to try. Some of my readers and students have asked me if it's necessary to incorporate all of the practices and rituals I've laid out in this book into their lives, as it seems daunting, even off-putting, to be asked to do so much. The answer is, of course not. I'm not at all suggesting you assimilate everything I've laid before you. Some tools and rituals will appeal to you and others won't. Consider the suggestions in the book much like offerings at a buffet. They are simply options for you to enjoy. Also, the beauty of a buffet is that you get to sample a little of everything before deciding what you love and want to load onto your plate.

In the same spirit, I suggest that you try all of the rituals, as the ones you're tempted to dismiss or ignore might very well turn out to be the ones that yield the deepest, most profound, even life-changing, results and insights. So, be open, give everything a try, and see what happens. The good news is that most of these attunement practices and rituals are so simple that to do them is not difficult or time consuming. Some, in fact, are quite intriguing and engaging—even downright fun—and set you up to have many surprising assists from your intuition throughout each day without even trying. View each practice or ritual as a means of better tuning in to the frequency of your intuition and Spirit, much like better tuning in to a specific radio station. With a small shift comes clear guidance.

## Patience Please

Be patient as you learn how to tune in to your intuition for guidance. It may seem elusive at first, but one day—and it may be sooner than you think—everything will suddenly just click and you'll find yourself flowing automatically with the unconditionally loving, unlimited guidance of your Spirit. I suggest you read each chapter slowly and not rush through the book. Unless, of course, you can't help yourself, in which case go ahead and read it all, but then go back to the beginning and read it again more slowly, answering the questions in order, trying not to skip any, followed by actually attempting the simple practices I suggest.

The reason I encourage you not to skip answering the questions is because I've found that the ones you're most tempted to skip or feel have no relevancy tend to have the greatest potential to open you up to some of the most profound intuitive insight and guidance available. So please do be curious and patient enough to answer all of the questions at the end of each section, even the ones that don't seem to apply to you at all.

## Be Honest

The most significant and necessary challenge you will face when tuning in to your intuition is to be completely honest with yourself and others. This isn't necessarily an easy or clear assignment, especially for those who have been conditioned to hide, suppress, or ignore their feelings all their lives. I've found that a powerful way to help focus on your honest feelings is to write about them on a regular basis, rather than just mentally reflecting on them in your head. Writing seems to open up the truth serum in your heart and gets it flowing in a way that just thinking never will. Therefore, I strongly encourage you to keep a journal exclusively dedicated to answering the questions within the chapters. It's worth the effort.

When tuning in to your intuition, you will find that once you name it, you claim it. In other words, once you openly acknowledge your intuition, it's almost impossible to ignore, and writing down your feelings is one of the most powerful ways to do this. Your journal will soon hold solid evidence that your intuition is a valuable resource worth listening to.

## Write It Down

Your rational mind might tempt you to rush through the questions in the book, even be impatient with them, rather than encourage you to dig deeply enough to find true answers. Allowing your ego to stop you from journaling your answers will trip you up and rob you of the important insights your intuition holds for you. The more you take the time to write down your answers, the more the voice of your Spirit will start to come through loud and clear . . . and surprise you with tremendously helpful guidance than merely mentally perusing these questions will ever reveal.

Even more important, when writing down your answers you will begin to sense the significant difference in tone and energy, in *vibration* or *feel,* between your intuition and your ego. The wisdom of your intuition, when it comes through, feels more honest, more grounded, more expanded, and above all, unarguably more true *for you* in the deepest core of your being than your fearful, guarded ego ever will. When writing down the answers to the questions within each section, pay attention to this energetic difference so that when your intuition communicates with you during the day, you quickly recognize its vibration and are therefore far more prepared to follow it in the moment of decision. The exercises in this book are specifically designed to help you become more attuned to your Spirit and stop being someone you aren't. So give the questions a chance *on paper* and discover this for yourself.

### The Power of Daily Rituals

If you want your intuition to guide you in life, you have to practice listening to it, plain and simple. Much like radio waves constantly being broadcasted, your Spirit is constantly broadcasting to your conscious mind through your intuition. But if you are not tuned in, you will miss it.

My greatest gift in life was learning early on to tune in to my intuition and allow my Spirit to guide me in every aspect of my life. As a child, I was given several daily rituals to follow to make listening to my intuition the foundation and safeguard of my existence. Through years and years of repeating these simple rituals every day, they're now woven into the very fabric of who I am.

One of these daily rituals for tuning in to my Spirit for guidance, for example, was introduced to me when I was in Catholic elementary school and reinforced years later while I was a high-school student working with my first intuitive mentor, Charlie Goodman. This ritual was to recite the Lord's Prayer—the Our Father—out loud first thing every morning upon waking. I started doing this in the first grade, when I was not quite six years old, and it's still part of my regular morning routine. Saying this prayer, among other things, quiets my mind, opens my heart, and deeply connects me to my Spirit. Reciting it aloud leaves me feeling grounded, balanced, and receptive to guidance as I begin a new day.

Another daily ritual I learned from my mother when I was again no more than six or seven years old. Before I go to sleep each night, I thank, out loud in prayer, my spiritual guides, ancestors, guardian angels, and all unseen spirit helpers known and unknown for the assistance, support, protection, and blessings they bestowed upon me throughout the day. By thanking God and my unseen helpers, I maintain a grateful heart, which is another essential for receiving guidance and living in flow. A third ritual I've followed since childhood is to ask often (again, out loud) for guidance, assistance, and support from my Divine Self and all spirit helpers in the unseen world throughout each day. Thanks to this simple ritual, I've never felt I was "going it alone" in the world. I've always felt—and have been—supported and protected as I move through each day, as though I have an entourage of spirit guides and angelic bodyguards surrounding and helping me all day long. I do.

These are just three of the many simple rituals I practice every day to stay tuned in to my intuition and my Spirit. All my rituals have become cherished parts of my being. Some rituals I've kept the same, doing them exactly as I was taught to, and others have evolved over the years through my own creativity. The constant, however, is that not a day begins, unfolds, or ends without me tuning in to my intuition, listening to my Spirit, expressing gratitude, being absolutely open and receptive to help, and asking the great Creator—the Giver of all life—to direct me to my greatest good and highest service.

So how do you remain tuned in to your joyous, loving, guiding Spirit when life might be more challenging than ever? There is only one way to succeed and that is to make getting in touch with your Spirit the most important thing in your life. Your intuition is the pulse, the voice, and the light of your most authentic Self and is the only thing that can successfully lead you to find and happily experience all that you seek.

Tuning in to your intuition and listening to your Spirit should become as automatic as brushing your teeth or taking a shower. And that comes with practicing small daily rituals, including conscious breathing, meditation, setting your intention, paying attention to the moment, listening more deeply to your heart, expressing gratitude, acknowledging your successes, and most of all, surrendering to the flow of your inner guidance as it arises. With daily rituals you'll begin to quickly tap into your intuition more often and more clearly. Next, you will start to trust it, and soon you will find yourself acting on it as it serves to guide you each day.

Just as plugging a computer into an electrical source gives it the power it needs to run, we, too, must "plug in" to our source of inner power, our inner guidance, which is centered in our heart. Without such rejuvenating contact with our inner Self, we become depleted of Spirit and our lives reflect this emptiness. For example, I know individuals—and you may, as well—who seem to have it all (at least on a material level, living prosperous, comfortable lives) but are still deeply unhappy because they're out of touch with their Spirit. Others feel this loss of contact with their Spirit but try to fill the void through drinking, drugging, gambling, having meaningless sex, and more.

With daily rituals in place to connect us with our inner voice and Spirit, we recharge from within, which gives us greater confidence, better direction, deeper insight, and expanded creativity. Through the practice of rituals such as quiet breathing, taking specific time out to listen to our heart, sitting in front of our altar or adding something new and meaningful to it once in a while, our soul stays in better alignment with our true purpose in life. Daily rituals ease us into the habit of tuning in and keeping us centered there.

## Give Things a Chance

Take your time as you move from fear to flow. Implement at least one of the daily practices or simple rituals at the end of each section and give it a fair chance to work. Start by trying a practice for two or three days. If you have a positive experience, continue the practice for a week, then two weeks, and then three. Studies show that it takes about 40 days for a new habit to develop and become part of your life, so keep the 40-day goal in mind. We don't change overnight, even if we want to, and while I'd love to suggest that you can quickly tune in to your intuition in a few short steps, to remember to implement them in your life and make it part of who you are takes a little more time.

What I can tell you is that a few simple rituals or practices kept up for the duration of 40 days will change your life. As you'll see, the practices are easy enough to do, and some take no more than a single breath. The challenge is to perform them regularly and consistently. You are changing the lifelong habit of tuning out your inner guidance to one of tuning it in, and daily practice is the only way you will succeed. These rituals and practices help establish a new way of being, one in which you listen to your heart over your fears. The good news is that doing each practice or ritual also has the added benefit of relieving stress and anxiety, because the more you align with your Spirit, the more at peace you feel. At the very least, these practices will calm you down. At best, they will gracefully lead you back into the highest degree of flow with your Spirit and help you enjoy the best this life has in store for you.

### A Brand-New Day

If we make it our habit to tap into our greatest inner resource, our guiding Spirit, we start to experience life in surprisingly joyful, new ways. If we don't, we may enjoy an intuitive moment or two, but remain more often than not trapped by fear and mired in all the muck that comes with fear, such as anxiety, guilt, shame, flattery, bullying, being bullied, depression, and whatever else the ego resorts to when it feels threatened.

A client of mine named Anthony struggled with depression and insecurity that he covered up with a lot of false bravado, none of which those closest to him bought into, and he found himself arguing with his family and even friends at work more often than he cared to admit. It seemed nonstop at times, and although he officially told himself it was everyone else who was at fault, he secretly knew it was his defensiveness and overreactivity that caused most of the problems.

I felt guided to suggest to Anthony that he create an altar at home. I told him to place symbols of the things that he loved and cared about on it (more about this later in the book) and spend a few minutes in front of his altar every day as a ritual, breathing quietly and allowing himself to feel supported from within. At first he thought my suggestion was crazy, but it was quirky enough that he gave it a try anyway.

A few months later we spoke again, and he told me he had created a little altar in the backyard of his home and, in fact, even planted a garden in front of it so he had a reason to go out there, without looking weird to his family. Everyone thought he was just taking care of his garden. He managed to spend a few minutes in front of it most days, as he liked being out there. Anthony said that the ritual calmed him down, and the more time he spent there, the more he began sensing his inner voice telling him he could relax and not worry so much.

"I don't know why," he laughingly said, "but the more time I spent in front of my altar, the better behaved everyone else became, and I found myself getting in fewer fights." He winked at me. "It certainly has freed up some of the drama in my life, that's for sure, and I can't complain about that."

Another client, Ronald, began the ritual of writing down his intuitive feelings every day before he went to work. "The more I do this," he said, "the clearer my intuition is. What's so great, though, is because I write things down, I have proof that I'm not off base in what I sense. My journal is my evidence that I can trust my intuition. It's crazy," he laughed, then continued more seri-ously, "without writing things down like you suggested, I would never have been able to trust myself the way I do now. And my life is working out better than ever for it. Thank God!"

As you practice daily rituals to touch base with your inner voice, as Ronald and Anthony did, the more you'll experience the magic of intuition. Synchronicity replaces struggle. Doors sudden-ly open instead of close. Your relationships begin to improve in-stead of break down, and life generally becomes more alive, even joyful.

### Making the Shift

Trusting and following your Spirit over your fears is a huge shift for most people and takes more than a mental decision to fully embody. Such a transformational shift requires an entire re-ordering of your life. You must want to make this shift so intense-ly that you are willing to rearrange your priorities a little, examine and change your beliefs one at a time as needed, patiently imple-ment new habits and behaviors, and allow your Spirit to influence you on a daily basis. You must turn away from the outside world for affirmation and go within to find it. By this I mean choose to listen to the deep, inner you over the outer world, and be open and vulnerable enough to say so and act on your intuition. You may meet with resistance from within and criticism from out-ward, but none will be greater than the power of your true Self when it's in charge.

Once you decide to commit to a more authentic, intuitive way of being, the path is surprisingly straightforward. It simply involves establishing a new set of personal priorities and commit-ting to the daily practice of surrendering yourself to the guidance of the Spirit within. Once you do so, the resulting positive person-al experiences you'll have will provide the motivation to continue. Each day that you surrender to your inner guidance is a day you live as an authentic and lighthearted being, rather than another day you endure as an anxiously controlled and fearful soul.

The following chapters serve as your guide through each of these exciting steps of intuitive empowerment. They will assist your return to a life guided by your loving, authentic Spirit. Remember to take your time and savor each step, for they all bear tremendous gifts. As you progress, you can look forward to the return of your limitless power and light.

✳

There's just one more thing I want to share before we begin. I'm writing this book as much for myself (or at least for my "ego self") as for you. I too am learning and growing as I continue to surrender my fears even more, and it is my authentic Spirit writing through me that has filled these pages . . . so I've been especially interested in what has come through!

Every one of us is at a different level of growing into a higher, more conscious being during these transformational times. We're learning and growing together. Each story I share in this book is my own, or comes by way of my clients and friends, and is intended to honestly reflect the challenges we face in learning to flow as Divine beings. We all have a piece to contribute to the great puzzle of transformation, because there is only one Spirit in which we all live, breathe, and exist. As we each effect positive change as individuals, at the same time we're helping others find their way home, too.

It is my sincere wish and prayer that we all experience a grounded, guided journey from head to heart, from frustration to flow. May we feel the presence of Spirit within, and remember and witness the Holy Spirit in each other, knowing that we are all returning to our true and holy nature. And may we resist the urge to turn back in fear, however tempting it may be in the moment.

*Author's note:* All of the stories in this book are true. However, all names have been changed (other than my own name or those of my family members) to protect the privacy of the individuals involved.

✳   ✳   ✳

# Chapter Two

# STEP ONE: WAKING UP

We often find ourselves arriving at this first step of transformation being relatively unconscious of and/or even uninterested in the spiritual nature of the earth or ourselves. Our attention is usually outwardly oriented and focused more on the physical world around us than on the world within. We may feel hurried, irritable, and stressed out, even in a low-grade state of emergency over one thing or another. We see life as a challenge and meet each new day prepared for battle. We are tense and often unconsciously holding our breath and forgetting to breathe deeply, which creates an inner state of anxiety, a feeling of "fight-or-flight" in the body.

Before we embrace our intuition as the guiding force in our life, we have a tendency to seek direction, approval, and even our identity mostly from the people around us and are more often followers rather than leaders. If we do lead, we may find ourselves doing so by consciously or unconsciously instilling some form of fear in others so that they comply, mostly because we're living in fear ourselves. We tend to manage our lives intellectually—in other words, we get stuck in our heads, keeping ourselves preoccupied with juggling an assortment of activities and responsibilities in order to manage the surface of life. Meanwhile, underneath we feel empty, hungry for meaning, restless, somewhat lost, and frequently ungrounded—as if we aren't really inhabiting our own bodies. This is why we keep ourselves so busy. It's one way to distract ourselves, at least temporarily, from experiencing the low-grade inner anxiety that haunts us.

### Change . . . for the Better

Most of us get caught up in this spiritually unconscious state at one time or another, depending on our overall soul development. But no matter where we are on our soul's journey toward a life of purpose, this state of slumber usually comes to an abrupt end. We're often forced to wake up to a need for deeper self-awareness by some sort of highly unexpected or hugely upsetting crisis, such as being in an accident, getting an illness, losing a loved one, or feeling rejected by someone we love. Our unconscious or complacent state can also come to an unexpected end as the result of losing a job, graduating from college, leaving a marriage or long-term relationship, starting a new relationship (the loss of single life), or having children (the end of being childless). No matter what actual event or circumstance makes us wake up to the fact that the way we're living isn't working or has to change, these incidents force us to turn inward and look deeper than we are accustomed to for guidance, reassurance, grounding, and new direction.

Waking up to the possibility of living life guided by intuition can be exciting, but it can also be disturbing—at least from the ego mind's point of view—so sometimes we might be tempted to continue as if everything were the same. Once our yearning for deeper awareness begins, however, we cannot ignore it for long. Like a crack in a door opening to an entirely new wing of ourselves and the universe we inhabit, the hidden aspects of our lives and ourselves begin calling and we're ultimately compelled to explore.

Once we begin to awaken to our intuition, our Spirit, we sense possibilities in life that we weren't aware of before and want to find out what they are. As if waking up from a dream, we start to look at our world with fresh eyes and a newfound sense of curiosity. We begin to wonder, perhaps for the first time, if there really is more than meets the eye in our life, and if so, we want to know what it is!

Like Humpty Dumpty, once you awaken to the calling of your Spirit, the world as you know it shatters—never to be reassembled again. And yet it comes as no genuine surprise that it was merely a shell that hid from you a much deeper and more expansive reality that leads to greater potential for fulfillment and inner peace.

So if you're awakening to a need to look deeper within and watching your old world fall apart, don't struggle to put it back together. Instead, trust that the disruption will lead you to a more authentic sense of Self and purpose once the dust settles. Rather than cling to what wasn't true and fulfilling to your Spirit, sift among the pieces for the parts that do feel genuine. Look for what might reflect your true Spirit, and hold on to only those aspects. While it may be difficult to accept, all disruptions in life are part of your spiritual awakening, and in the end are set in motion in response to your own internal craving to connect with your true power and authentic inner voice.

For example, I have a client named Patricia, who was in remission from a particularly rare form of breast cancer and was understandably fearful that it would come back. In addition, she was in a terrible second marriage to a man she knew was an alcoholic but was afraid to confront him, although she desperately wanted him to move out so she could relax and focus on her health. Moreover, he told her that he'd had an affair for the entire time she was in treatment, which totally disgusted and shattered Patricia, leaving her wondering what was solid in her life.

"I know having him around isn't good for me, but I've already divorced once," she shared, "and I worry that people will think I'm such a failure. I feel really guilty that I became sick, and even blame myself for his affair. As crazy as it sounds, I also worry about what will happen to him. We fight almost every day because of his drinking, and now over the affair, but I'm not sure it's right to ask him to leave."

"Patricia," I answered, "rather than have me tell you what to do with him, which I won't, ask your Spirit for guidance. What does your intuition say?"

She was quiet for all of ten seconds, and then said, "I know it's time for him to go."

"No, Patricia. That isn't your inner guidance speaking," I replied. "That is your reasoning mind. I can tell by your resignation. Now check in again. Go to your heart and listen. What does your Spirit say?"

This time she was quiet for much longer. Finally she answered. "My Spirit says to ask him to leave today. If I don't, I won't be able to find the peace I need to stay well for myself and for my kids, no matter how disruptive it may be for now."

"How do feel you about this awareness?" I asked.

Again she was quiet for a time, and I could sense she was checking in with herself for the answer. Finally she took a breath and then spoke. "I actually feel relieved," she answered, sounding surprised. "I know it's right for me, and I'm just holding on because I don't want to face his reaction, or the judgment and embarrassment that I might have to deal with from my family. The truth is, I've wanted him out for a while. I even wonder at times if my deep unhappiness with him contributed to my illness in the first place. I wouldn't doubt it. Being with him has made me feel sick for a long time."

I didn't answer. I actually didn't need to say anything more to Patricia at that moment. I could tell she was tuned in to her inner voice, and because of that I knew she would follow through and take care of herself, even if it did temporarily invite more disruption into her life.

Several months later Patricia contacted me again. She shared that she had, in fact, asked her husband to move out the day we last spoke, and because he could feel her resolve, he surprisingly agreed. He went further downhill for several months, then quite spontaneously checked himself into a rehabilitation facility and was on his way back to sobriety. They were now attending counseling together, something else he would never agree to do before they were separated.

"I have no idea if I will get back together with him," she shared. "It was hell living with him, and I hated it for a long time. And it's been a real challenge to meet life head-on without him, but I'm doing it. What's best of all is that I can see my asking him to move wasn't just good for me. It was good for him as well, and he has admitted as much. Once in therapy he even said he kept pushing me to see how far he could go, which made me angry. At least I no longer feel guilty about asking him to leave. I'm so glad I got past my fear and trusted my Spirit. It's clear that beyond all the upset going on, we're both better off for the change."

When we wake up to our inner Self, we realize that whatever disruptions and upsets we face in life don't just gratuitously happen to us—although it may certainly feel that way. Rather, on a soul level, *our call to greater alignment with our true Self invites change and disruption to occur, or at least uses all loss and upset as an opening to move into deeper contact with our Divine Spirit, the conscious creator of our life.*

### Get On Board

As you begin to wake up to a deeper sense of Self, take heart in knowing that you're not alone in this disruptive journey of spiritual transformation. Even those who are already on a spiritual path will experience disruption as they, too, move into even more direct contact with their inner guidance and Divine Spirit. We are all works in endless progress. As long as we are in human form, achieving deeper levels of inner awareness, intuition, and higher levels of spiritual consciousness and personal creative power is our purpose.

Disruptive awakening is your signal that you're ready to take the initial step toward attaining your authentic identity and moving into a more deeply guided awareness of your personal path and purpose in life. While awakening experiences are often unexpected, and even scary, in truth they are invitations from your Spirit to remember and begin living at the highest level of your inner truth. The key is to trust that you are ready and know in your heart and soul that this is what you want more than any other thing.

Just as it feels intimidating on the first day of school no matter what grade you're in—from kindergarten to college—the first day on a new spiritual journey can be equally nerve-wracking. Just know that when you find yourself in conditions that ask you to wake up to your Spirit, you are at this junction because on a soul level you've worked your way here and you *are* prepared to enter a new way of being, even if it feels uncomfortable or threatening or overwhelming at first.

When life falls apart in some unexpected way or challenges you to embrace sudden, often painful change, it's because you've progressed to the point where the things you've held on to as false security blankets no longer serve you; and you're longing to live a deeper, more intuitively guided life of authentic spiritual power and purpose. When change is upon you, know without a doubt that you're ready to let go of present limitations, be they in the form of relationships, ideas, circumstances, and most of all, beliefs so that you might start to live from a place of deeper truth, power, and meaning.

### A Deeper Awareness

I often ask people I work with if they were genuinely surprised when their wake-up call came. Almost everyone I've spoken to has said something like: "On the surface, yes . . . but deep down, no, I wasn't surprised. I even felt it coming. I just didn't know when or how. And honestly, I'm glad it did, even if it was difficult and painful to get through at first."

These reflections ring true for me, as well. I've also experienced many unexpected and deeply disruptive awakening moments that took my breath away and caught me off guard, some of the biggest in the recent past. For example, I experienced the sudden death of both my brother and father only six weeks apart. I broke my kneecap in an injury I sustained while working out at the gym and had to have surgery that left me in a wheelchair for five months. I've also recently experienced betrayal in more than one significant relationship, with people who have been in my life for many years. But in my heart of hearts, I know these events occurred either in direct response to my soul's yearning to live an even more authentic way, or were an invitation from the Universe for me to do so. My soul was presented these challenges to support my continuing transformation into my fullest Divine expression.

For most of us, what is most shocking is how unexpected our soul awakening experiences can be. For example, I never expected to end such long-term relationships or experience the devastation of two back-to-back deaths in my family, let alone find myself confined to a wheelchair for so long. All of these events swooped in on me when I wasn't looking and caught me by surprise. And yet, such are the nature of soul-examining wake-up calls. They often catch us unaware and humble us in such a way that our intellect (or ego) cannot explain away, minimize, or silence their impact. Once a call to Spirit sounds in your heart or pulls the rug out from beneath your feet, you're compelled to sit up, pay attention, and listen. Like waking up to an earthquake in the middle of the night, you simply can't go back to sleep.

When your life is touched by this deep disturbance of the old status quo, be glad. It's an answer to a prayer, even if it first presents as your worst nightmare. No matter how challenged you may find yourself, have faith in the Universe and trust that behind it all, you are being invited to open up to something far more beautiful than your limited ego-based perceptions will allow or can create: the kind of profound life experience you deeply long for and intuitively know you deserve.

## Room to Breathe

A common wake-up call is feeling as though you are living in an endless state of emergency and cannot seem to break free. You might feel anxious, even threatened, as though you have a band of tigers on your tail and are running out of the energy you need to stay one step ahead of the danger. A key tool for breaking free of this condition and allowing yourself to live without such a sense of urgency is to take a deep breath and pay attention to where you are right now, in this very moment. Such internal states of emergency are the result of trying to breathlessly manage or control a perceived future danger or are the result of trying to create a different outcome in what is now a past disappointment in order to feel better, neither of which is possible, thus adding to this vicious cycle of stress and fear.

I recently spoke with my client Cynthia, who had endured one of the most tumultuous years of her life. Without warning she'd lost her job of 23 years working as a small-business loan officer for a local bank that was taken over by a larger one. On the day she was let go, her boss and dear friend (or so she thought) unceremoniously gave her a very small severance package and then told her she had to clear her desk and be gone in an hour. His cold treatment of her left her feeling as though she had been betrayed in every way. After all, this was someone she had worked side by side with for years—someone she had laughed and joked with, eaten lunch with, and shared family milestones with, such as the birth of his children and the marriage of her daughter. His detached indifference in letting her go was more painful to experience than losing the job itself. Shocked, she felt utterly dumped, and it broke her heart.

Shortly after this devastation Cynthia's husband, Joe, an accountant in a large firm, was informed that his job, too, was being phased out. In his case, however, he was offered an equal position in another state, but if he accepted the offer, he would have to move in less than two weeks. Given that the job market was so bleak in their city and the prospects of finding local work in his capacity seemed nearly impossible, he felt forced to accept. Cynthia agreed that they needed his income given her loss of a job, so she supported his decision to take the job and helped him pack. Even though she saw the need for this move and was grateful for his continued employment, his sudden departure felt to Cynthia like yet another big loss, leaving her emotionally bereft and depleted. All this stress took a huge toll on her health, and she started experiencing severe back pain that only seemed to go from bad to worse to absolutely unbearable.

She consulted numerous back specialists and tried endless therapies, from chiropractic to massage, in search of relief from the excruciating pain she was now suffering nonstop. An MRI revealed a slipped disc, and she was advised to undergo surgery to bring relief. Against her better judgment she agreed and ended up having two surgeries on her back, both of which rendered little relief, leaving her more demoralized than ever.

In spite of these challenges, Cynthia was a true warrior, and in her quest to end this downward spiral, she managed to secure a temporary position in a new company as a training director, which promised to turn into something permanent if she proved herself on the project she was hired to do. Thrilled not to be unemployed, she hobbled to work every day hoping to hide just how debilitated she was, and she fought the good fight against her back pain with large doses of Advil and Bengay ointment.

Getting into her car on the very morning we spoke, Cynthia realized she hadn't taken a moment to herself in days, maybe weeks, and even our conversation had to be cut short because she was running late for several appointments. Life seemed like an endless state of emergency that she was managing well enough, but the toll of the tremendous stress she was under was exhausting. Underneath it all she was frightened of losing control of her life completely. Cynthia wondered how much longer she could go on before she'd collapse.

Cynthia's story is similar to so many other people's experiences that I've been hearing about lately. They're barely managing to get through these rocky times, facing one loss after another, and it seems to be turning into an epidemic. When I asked Cynthia if she felt safe, she laughed out loud.

"No!" she replied vehemently. "Not now—not at all—probably not ever if I think about it." Then she paused and asked very sincerely, "Is it even possible to feel safe enough to relax in this world?"

"Not really," I answered. "At least not in the way you're physically responding to everything coming at you. Naturally you've been threatened by all this upheaval, and it's taking your breath away. As long as you aren't breathing through all of this change and challenge in a deeper, more grounded way, your body can't relax and catch up. Being breathless leaves you braced for the next blow, so to speak, and this is contributing to the pain in your back.

"As a matter of fact," I continued, "I've spoken with several alternative health-care practitioners over the years who have suggested to me that a lot of people's back pain stems from holding fear in the body rather than releasing it, which can be done through deep, relaxing breathing. It's not that you can't catch up or keep up or get ahead, Cynthia. It's just that you won't be able to do it without breath."

In the midst of facing her formidable challenges, she had allowed her breath to be taken away. I could tell because, as I listened to her, I was starting to resonate with her breathless energy, and it was beginning to take my breath away, as well. As sentient beings, whether we recognize it or not, we are deeply affected by the energy of the people around us, especially the powerful energy of fear and anxiety. If we aren't aware of it, we begin to take on other people's emotional states and internalize them as our own. No doubt about it, like a toxic cloud, when disconnected from our breath and our Spirit, we really stress each other out! Catching myself, I pulled the phone away from my ear for a moment and took a breath so that I could stay centered and remain intuitively receptive and free from her contagious anxiety.

"Breathe, Cynthia," I gently coached, "If you aren't breathing well you can't relax and get grounded in the midst of all this upheaval, let alone tune in to your intuition. And your body will remain tense and cause more pain in your back."

"Moreover," I continued, "if you don't remember to breathe deeply, you disconnect from your Spirit, your inner guidance, and your authentic personal power. And that is what feels so threatening."

At first Cynthia resisted. Taking a deep breath required her to let down her defenses, which was hard for her to do, but I insisted. After a bit more hesitation she did finally take in one, then two, then three deep breaths. As she did, I could feel the tension start to drain out of her body right through the phone, replaced with a sense of expanded space, literally the "room to breathe."

After a few moments of my encouraging her simply to breathe, I asked Cynthia how she felt. "Calmer. Quiet," she answered. "Better." Encouraged by the shift in her energy, I asked her if she still felt as threatened as she had only moments earlier.

"Well, I wouldn't say I feel entirely safe enough to relax, but something inside tells me that the worst is over, and I'll be okay. That's a relief."

I wasn't surprised that she experienced such a significant shift in only a few breaths. As though changing the channel of her mind from fearful thoughts to calming Spirit, that "something" she referred to sensing inside was an intuitive realization that underneath the surface waves of reactive stress and fear she was experiencing, she was in fact safe enough to relax and would not lose control of her life as she had feared.

As I shared with Cynthia, breathing deeply is the most fundamental and important way to tune in to your Spirit and get grounded in the midst of chaos. It's essential to breathe deeply in order to tune in to what is real and tune out what is false. When we hold our breath or breathe shallowly, we lose this basic connection to our Spirit. We become vulnerable to being overwhelmed by our own or others' fearful thoughts and imaginings, pulling us into unwanted fight-or-flight or freeze states. Once we reconnect with our breath, we are able to access our deeper knowing and break free of vicious cycles of anxiety.

"Cynthia," I asked once she was recentered, "do you ever take a moment to check in with your intuition as you face all this chaos? You know, to help you move along more peacefully during the day?"

"No, not really," she replied. "I want to, but I forget. I mean, I know I should take time to go within, and I should try harder to listen to my intuition, but honestly, I'm so busy just keeping afloat that I just get caught up in everything flying at me . . . and before I know it, the day is over and I'm collapsing into bed once again. To tell you the truth, I don't really know what 'connecting to my intuition' means. How do you do that anyway?"

Now *that* was an honest and relevant question. Like so many others, Cynthia wanted to feel more guided and safe but had no idea how to make that happen. She'd picked up one or two spiritual books on intuition, including mine, and enjoyed them, but in spite of what she read, very little had changed in her life, except maybe that she now held the hope that change was possible. She wanted me to explain why things always remained the same.

The answer was clear to me, and I shared it with her. I told her that unless we give ourselves room to breathe and tune in to our intuition on a regular basis (and the key phrase is *regular basis*); unless we relax for a moment and listen to the subtle internal promptings of our heart that we all receive throughout the day, we risk remaining stuck in our anxious, fearful thinking . . . and nothing changes. Or, if it does change, we might not notice. Cynthia's life had changed in ways that she could manage, if only she gave herself a moment to appreciate this. Having room to breathe would help her physically relax and realize she had managed to carry on in spite of all the upset that had transpired, and this could bring relief to her back pain.

She was working and even liked her job; she was growing in new ways by developing her skills, and she actually found it refreshing to do something different. She planned to eventually join her husband in his new city but discovered that their temporary separation gave her some unexpected and welcome time alone, allowing her the ability to focus solely on herself as opposed to being in charge of them as a couple as she had been. Even her conversations with her husband were more alive than they had been in years. She was able to hear him as a person separate from her with his own challenges going on, something she had long tuned out. In the midst of their disruptions they were actually talking more, laughing more, and thereby strengthening their relationship.

"It's kind of like having a brand-new long-distance boyfriend," she laughingly admitted after she starting breathing more deeply. "In fact, I like our new arrangement for now because I only have to pay attention to him part time, and when I do, I enjoy him very much, all of which I cannot honestly say was happening for me over the past ten years."

Cynthia is like hundreds of people I've met all over the world. I firmly believe we all intuitively know in our hearts that there is a better way to live than being breathlessly controlled by fear and anxiety, but we often aren't yet aware enough, or uncomfortable enough, to finally stop and take a breath and open up that door to our own inner power. This drama and trauma of our awakening is the rumble before the storm, the shake before the quake that upsets the mind-numbing status quo and motivates us (or, more accurately, sometimes forces us) to stop the panic habit and tune in to our own higher awareness for direction and relief.

I had compassion for Cynthia for being so breathless because she, like most of us, lives in a society that rushes everything, and expects life to be delivered and problems resolved quickly. We order a pizza and it's at our doorstep in less than an hour. We go online and can purchase almost anything imaginable and have it delivered to our home with next-day shipping. We turn on the TV and have hundreds of channels to choose from. We're addicted to our BlackBerries, iPhones, iPads, and other technical devices that keep us wired to the outer world . . . but how are we supposed to focus on, let alone tune in to, the inner world?

We don't live in a culture that's supportive of slowing down, listening to our intuition and following it, let alone encouraging us to take a deep enough breath to tune inward in the first place. If anything, our world is designed to keep us completely tuned out, to laugh at or ignore our inner Self altogether, numbing us with lousy substitutes that keep us addicted and dependent on more and more "false gods of technology" of the external world.

The preamble to our intuitive awakening is often marked by sudden change or a growing sense of overwhelm, exhaustion, anxiety, restlessness, impatience, irritation, depression, and dissatisfaction in our lives at the deepest level. In other words, it's a feeling that life is a struggle, we have no way to make it different, and there's nothing we can do about it. This isn't true. Take a deep breath right now, then another, and another; and you will discover this for yourself.

### Tuning In

Our ego mind often resists change for fear of losing control, and so it will do everything in its power to avoid it. Fears such as "I might lose my job," "I might end up alone," "I won't be able to pay my bills," or "People will abandon me," take over and seem real. That's why so many of us remain stuck, telling ourselves that we want a spiritual change yet doing little to nothing about it. We have the best intentions of going within and listening to our inner voices for guidance, but often fail to actually take a single step on the road to becoming an intuitively awakened being. We promise ourselves that we'll read the spiritual books that have been given to us by those who have heard our complaints, or that we've bought on our own accord, but we rarely get through more than a chapter or two before being swept back into the same old patterns of drama and struggle.

We promise ourselves we will go deeper and look within but soon forget—that is, until life becomes so frustrating or painful or circumstances change so much that we can no longer stay the same. Talking to others about how unhappy we are, even genuinely expressing the desire to experience the peace and personal power that comes from honoring our guiding Spirit, is only that: all talk and no action.

Unless and until we take *specific and regular action* starting with giving ourselves room to breathe, and directly tuning in to our intuition and listening to our Spirit every day, day after day—until it becomes the central foundation of our lives—sadly, little will change.

Being caught up in the rat race of trying to control everything is the way most of us have been taught to approach life thus far, and even I admit, it can be seductive. When you're on top of the wheel, and things are going your way it feels like you're competing. The mental game of "keeping things under control" may even give you a temporary sense of power, especially when you're accomplishing things, which is why it can be so enthralling. You may feel a temporary high, an adrenaline rush, which leaves you momentarily satisfied. It's as if you're winning the game . . . but are you, really?

You know the answer. It certainly feels seductive when the wheel is turning your way, but it's quite different when you fall under the wheels of life or get thrown off the wheel altogether as Cynthia was when she lost her job, a lifelong friendship, the company of her husband, and her physical well-being.

That's when you know the mental game of control has its limits. Enjoy it if it's working, but know that at the root of this approach to life is fear, and it will eventually takes its toll. Also know there is a better way to live, one that invites you to step off the rat-race wheel and tune in to your inner voice for direction and guidance, affirmation and support.

When we allow ourselves to take a breath and tune inward rather than be controlled by external forces, to follow our intuition and listen to our Spirit, we stop battling with life. With breath we move away from fight, flight, or freeze; and we end the struggle with ourselves, each other, and even with time. The more we allow ourselves room to breathe, the more life starts breathing with us, and everything feels better.

### Asking the Questions

Close your eyes and calmly breathe in and out through your nose. Start with a sigh or two to help you relax. Massage your jaw and throat a little to release even more tension and fear held in that part of your body, your expression center. Feel the energetic tension that your racing mind creates in your body. Do you notice how it drains your energy, your life force, your kefi, right out of you?

Now relax the tension in your neck and throat as much as possible with a few gentle stretches and take in a deep, easy, belly-filling breath. Don't force your breath to enter your body by raising your shoulders and holding your head back. Rather, keep your shoulders comfortably relaxed and down, and allow your belly to pull the air in naturally without any tension at all. Exhale by releasing the sound "Ah," and then bring the corners of your lips up to your ears in a gentle smile.

Next, take out your journal and tune inward. Contemplate each of the following questions, and invite your intuition, your guiding Spirit, your most authentic Self, to respond to each one. Give yourself plenty of time to feel the genuine response coming from your heart, the source of your power.

- What changes or challenges, expected or unexpected, are you presently facing?

- Who or what situation are you presently struggling with the most?

- In what area overall do you feel the greatest stress or worry? How long have you felt this?

- Do you feel you have enough time in your daily routine to tune in to your intuition and listen to your heart? What takes up most of your day?

- On a scale of 1 to 10, how much of a "state of emergency" are you generally in? Is this a reflection of present conditions, or is this a feeling you've carried longer in your life?

- What causes a "state of emergency" in you most often?

- How is your physical health? Do you have any serious or chronic aches and pains?

- How is your energy level? Do you have enough energy during the day, or do you often feel exhausted?

- Do you sleep well? Do you get enough sleep each night? Do you wake up feeling rested?

- Do you have the time to do the things you love? Do you remember what you love? Can you name the things you love right now? Do you follow through to engage in what you love?

- What thoughts, worries, fears, and/or people are you trying to control?

- Who or what is controlling you?

After writing down your answers, set your journal aside and take another deep, relaxing breath. As you exhale, let all of your tension go by again releasing the sound "Ah," and simply *be* for a moment or two, even longer if possible. Enjoy sitting and breathing deeply, empty of all thought, free of any agenda, any rush, and in the moment. Feel this vibration of being connected to your Spirit, your true and holy Self, through your breath. Notice how peaceful, content, and even energized you feel when you breathe deeply, tune inward, and focus on your Spirit. This is the source of your real power. It's available to you at all times. It is the real you guiding you right now. *Remember this.*

### *Daily Ritual: Notice the Moment*

Slow down and breathe easier. Unless you're escaping from a fire, there's no need to be in emergency mode. Slowly inhale through your nose, placing your tongue on the roof of your mouth as you do, keeping your mouth closed, and exhale loudly through your nose, almost as if breathing like Darth Vader from *Star Wars*. Repeat this several times whenever you feel stressed, anxious, or uneasy. This breathing technique eases tension and calms and quiets your mind so you feel more grounded and relaxed.

Next, set your alarm on your cell phone to go off twice a day. When it beeps (or chirps, vibrates, or whatever type of alarm setting you prefer), stop what you're doing and look around. No matter what is going on, take that moment to notice exactly where you are. Identify the details, saying them out loud if possible or under your breath if necessary. What colors, shapes, people, buildings, or animals do you see? Listen to your surroundings. Do you hear others talking, a radio blaring, birds singing, a distant siren? Notice the textures of the things touching your body. What kind of surface are you standing or sitting on? Do you feel a warm or cool breeze on your cheeks? Inhale the scents filling the air. Do you smell coffee brewing, food cooking, or perhaps fresh flowers sitting in a vase? Look in the distance. Is there a smoky haze across the horizon? Bright sunshine streaming through the window? High-rise buildings or trees all around? Continue to gently breathe while experiencing and expanding each of your senses. Observation is the gateway to intuition, a direct link to your Spirit.

The mind often races back and forth between the past and future, therefore noticing very little in the moment, but the awake and aware guiding Spirit embodies the now. When your mind isn't focused in the present moment, it can't accurately read the energy of the moment, so it cannot guide you at all. I know it's easy to get preoccupied with reliving events in the past and worrying about events to come, leaving you distracted and unable to give your full attention to the present. However, in order to tune in to your intuition, you need to learn what you need to learn from the past and then move on, and realize that by paying attention to the present, you'll be laying the groundwork for a better future.

Engage the power of your intuition and connect with your Spirit in this moment and choose the kind of experience you want to create today, focusing only on today, not worrying about tomorrow or next week or next month. Decide, rather than hope or wish, by stating out loud your intention for the day, and then ask your Spirit to guide you to make this happen. For example, you might say, "I intend to finish my project on time and without stress," or "I intend to make time for exercise and relaxation before dinner," or "I intend to speak with my parents without engaging in drama."

You are a Divine creator, and by asking your Spirit to guide you, and then tuning in to your intuition for direction, you can create and shape the life you choose to have by aligning your intuition with your intention. For example, you can intend to have an active business day filled with positive phone calls, appointments, and meetings; or perhaps you intend to create a joyful day filled with gratitude for your friends, family, co-workers, and all the people you interact with. You can successfully make this happen if you slow down, breathe, set an intention, and then pay attention to your intuition in the present moment as it guides you to these positive experiences.

### A Dead End

While it is important to live in the present, if we simply drift along focused only in the moment, without a sense of purpose or meaningful direction, we are often no better off than missing the present altogether. Unless we are present to something meaningful, we give up our capacity to create and end up wasting time. It's possible to drift through life, but if we're lucky, we'll experience a wake-up call that will rouse us from our trance and give us direction and focus.

Robert considered himself a "carefree creative," which really meant that he had no idea who he was or what he wanted to do with his life. At age 22, he had an open heart, a musical soul, and a sleeping Spirit. He didn't think about the future very often to the consternation of his father, who wanted his son to get a real job (preferably at the sawmill, where he worked) and begin a responsible life in earnest.

Instead, Robert spent his time playing conga drums in a band, taking occasional guitar lessons from friends, and living off quinoa and laughter. He wasn't serious about much of anything and mostly lived moment to moment—although there were times when, alone at night, he became very anxious and overwhelmed about his future, often causing him to worry or at least wonder what life had in store for him . . . or the fact that he was often broke and had no idea what he wanted to be or do when he grew up, if he ever did.

Nevertheless, each day seemed to somehow take care of itself. And other than being fairly hungry most days, Robert managed to get by and even have fun with his friends. That is, until one day he woke up with so much abdominal pain that he thought he was going to die. The next thing he knew, he was on his way to the hospital, where he was rushed into surgery to remove a burst appendix.

The next two weeks were spent in and out of consciousness, as his body was slow to heal. One morning, he woke up in a full sweat and fever, vomiting so violently that he nearly choked to death because he couldn't manage to sit up. The doctor on call immediately sent him back to surgery and reopened the incision where his appendix had been removed days earlier to discover that a stubborn infection had set in. Robert had to be treated with even more aggressive antibiotics in order to get it under control.

One night, shortly after the trauma of undergoing the second surgery, he slowly woke up out of his drug-induced daze to see an old Native American grandmother sitting next to him, holding his hand and gently stroking it as he lay there, barely able to move. Disoriented, he looked around the room, not sure where he was or what was happening, and saw several more ancient Native American women sitting near the window surrounded by a beautiful golden and pink halo of light. They all seemed to be watching over him.

Robert looked at the woman gently holding his hand. Although he was barely able to speak, he wanted to understand what was happening. "Grandmother, am I dead?" he asked in a whisper.

"No, Robert," she answered, patting his hand. "God has different plans for you," and said nothing more.

Disappointed because he felt so ready to leave his life, he closed his eyes and tried to connect to the reality of the situation. Still holding the old woman's hand, he suddenly heard another voice: "Robert? Robert? Are you okay?"

It was the night nurse, hovering over him, trying to wake him up. He hadn't rung for her or made any sound to call out for help, yet here she was all of a sudden. Her voice interrupted his connection to the old grandmother, almost as if she were preventing him from slipping out of his body and into death. He felt himself slowly returning to reality: to his hurting body, to the hospital bed, to this world, to his life. The grandmother's touch faded as did the presence of the other grandmothers sitting near the window, and all he could hold on to was her gentle voice in his head. Finally he opened his eyes.

The nurse looked concerned as she studied Robert. He could barely look up at her because he felt so weak, yet he somehow managed to whisper that he was all right. She waited and watched him for another moment, checked his temperature and reviewed his chart, straightened out his bedding, and then slowly left the room, gazing back one more time as if to be sure he was indeed okay.

Now fully awake, all that Robert could do was lie in bed and reflect on what he'd just experienced. Before his encounter with the grandmother, he was in overwhelming pain and had more than once prayed for death to end his suffering. There was nothing significant going on in his life to call him back, and he had no sense of direction or commitment to anything. In other words, he felt like he had nothing to lose by dying. It wasn't really a morose thought, as he definitely wasn't a sullen kind of guy. He just couldn't think of a valid reason to stay. Life felt like a dead end, and he wanted to move on.

However, after hearing the grandmother's words and feeling the gentle caress of her hand on his, a new feeling came over him. At first, he couldn't quite put his finger on it, but as he sat contemplating what had transpired, it became clear. It was a powerful belief that he suddenly did have a purpose to fulfill, and that God would oversee his life. Never before that moment had he felt such a strong sense of personal worth or that his life mattered . . . so much so that he was being watched over by the gentle, loving force of the grandmothers and that God was actually aware of his existence.

Robert briefly wondered if he'd dreamed the entire thing or if it was a drug-induced hallucination. It didn't matter, though. His experience was real to him, and it deeply impacted him. That night his world was transformed. He suddenly knew without a doubt that he would recover, and even more important, that his life would change for the better. He didn't know how, but he was absolutely certain that it would. He also felt a powerful fear that he'd always carried (but managed to suppress deep within) swiftly rise up and out of his body. It was gone. He was no longer worried about not having money or a life plan and was surprised by the intensity of the relief he experienced.

Three days later, Robert was released from the hospital and went home. Until then he had never once thought about his intuition, his inner voice, his Spirit or God, life and death, otherworldly helpers, or his purpose and mission. He had never pondered anything beyond the next moment, and this wasn't because he was content or confident about where he was going in life—rather, the unknown terrified and depressed him, a fact that he had pretended to ignore for years. Now that the veil between worlds had been pulled back and he was shown the great love and guidance available to him in so many unseen ways, Robert realized that he wanted to live in a more courageous, conscious way. He also didn't want to lose touch with the loving guidance that he had made contact with while between the worlds. He looked forward to the future and wanted to make a difference. He remembered what the grandmother had said to him and was committed to fulfilling the "plan" that God had for him.

Robert seemingly stepped back into the world as the same person who had entered the hospital—minus quite a few pounds, which left him looking rather skeletal—but he wasn't the same guy at all. Instead, he returned with a newly discovered, powerful awareness that there was far more to life and to himself, and a clear awareness of the Divine spirit helper who had spoken to him and assured him that he mattered and was loved. He became interested in all things spiritual and especially opened himself up to listening to the place in his heart, his intuition, where he felt a loving presence overseeing him. He still loved music and played every day, but an entirely new world had revealed itself to him and offered so much more.

It has now been 18 years since that night when Robert woke up in the hospital and was comforted by the grandmother's loving words. Since then, he committed to a healing practice in massage therapy, energy work, and breath work to assist others in accelerating their spiritual and intuitive awakening. The foundation of his healing practice is to help pull back the veil between this world and the spirit world so that other people can also feel the love and guidance that is always available to them.

Until that experience, Robert had been headed for a dead end. He truly believes that he "died" in the hospital that night and was mercifully reborn to the far more meaningful and grounded and intuitively guided life he loves today. The impact his spirit helper had on him caught him by surprise, especially because he wasn't aware of anything other than distracting himself from his fear up until she appeared. And yet, noticing how easily he could have continued to drift for years, with no true course of his own, he is humbled, amazed, and deeply grateful that a beautiful spirit guide did indeed intercede and speak to him and set him on the right path for him.

## *Tuning In*

Waking up to the spirit realm and all its subtle assistance is a necessary shift in harnessing your ability to live a fearlessly authentic life. We are not alone in the Universe; and unless we become intuitively aware of the many faces and levels of guidance available to help us, we cut ourselves off from Divine assistance, which often leads to fear, frustration, and dead ends.

There are so many guardians, healers, helpers, and teachers in the spirit realm who watch over us and keep us safe. Yet we cannot access their subtle healing support, nor can they influence us or add to our good, if we shut ourselves off from them. We must open our hearts and minds to the reality that the Universe is populated with countless benevolent beings of light who want to assist us. We're getting more and more evidence of this truth from the many people who have had near-death experiences and have come back to tell their tales. One compelling account of help from the spirit realm is found in a recently published book called *Proof of Heaven* by the Harvard-trained neurosurgeon Eben Alexander. Attacked by a virulent form of *E. coli* that caused severe meningitis, he languished in a coma. Because his brain was under attack for over six days, he was believed to be essentially brain dead. And yet, he woke up, miraculously intact, and fully recovered. Along with his recovery came a fascinating firsthand account of the unseen and unlimited loving realms of support available to us all on the other side of the veil. So with him, even our scientists are affirming the truth of our having unlimited support in the spirit world at all times. We just need to transcend our rigid and erroneous perceptions of the way things are and allow these loving spirits to come through and help us.

We may not see, hear, or touch our spirit guides, but their influence can be *felt* through a sudden "Aha!" moment—a breakthrough in insight, an inspired idea, a significant change of direction or heart, or a simple relinquishment of fear. That is how intuition, the voice of our inner teacher and supporters, speaks to us.

### Asking the Questions

Close your eyes and calmly breathe in and out through your nose. Start with a sigh or two to help you relax. Massage your jaw and throat a little to release even more tension and fear held in that part of your body, your expression center. Feel the energetic tension that your racing mind creates in your body. Do you notice how it drains your energy, your life force, your kefi, right out of you?

Now relax the tension in your neck and throat as much as possible with a few gentle stretches and take in a deep, easy, belly-filling breath. Don't force your breath to enter your body by raising your shoulders and holding your head back. Rather, keep your shoulders comfortably relaxed and down, and allow your belly to pull the air in naturally without any tension at all. Exhale by releasing the sound "Ah," and then bring the corners of your lips up to your ears in a gentle smile.

Next, take out your journal, turn your attention inward, and listen to your inner teacher and Divine supporters. Contemplate each of the following questions and invite your Spirit, your most authentic Self, to respond. Give yourself plenty of time to feel the genuine response coming from your heart, the source of your intuition.

- Have you ever suffered an injury, accident, or illness (physical, mental, or emotional) that seemed to impose a time-out from your ordinary world and wake you up to the more subtle, yet very real and powerful, realm of Spirit? Explain what happened in detail.

- Have you ever experienced a sudden intuitive revelation, an unexpected shift in perception, or a breakthrough in your worldview or understanding of the Spirit realm? Describe the circumstances.

- Have you ever been inexplicably rerouted or turned around once you knew in your heart you were pursuing a dead end? What happened?

- Have you ever experienced direct or indirect contact with spirit guides, departed family or friends, angels, or other spirit helpers either during a meditative state, an altered state, or a dream state?

- Have you ever had a sense of fear that was suddenly lifted and replaced with an inexplicable calmness?

- Have you ever felt guidance from a spirit guide? Can you remember its message to you? Did you take it to heart?

- Do you feel you are living by the inner guidance you've received, or have you slipped back into a more unconscious state of being that has forgotten the message or has let it fall to the wayside?

- Reflecting on your life today, are you open and receptive, or closed off from and relatively unaware of the subtle realm of Spirit around you?

- If your intuition were to offer you a guiding message this very moment, what do you imagine it would be? Write it down.

- Does this message have strong meaning for you? Does it resonate in your heart? Can it get past your intellectual resistance and sink in?

After writing down your answers, set aside your journal and remain seated. Close your eyes, and again calmly breathe in and out through your nose. Start with a sigh or two to help you relax. Massage around your eyes and forehead, even your cheeks, for a moment to further release tension and fear you may hold there. Release the sound "Ah," as you exhale. Pay attention to the vibration in your body as you focus on the more subtle realms of energy surrounding you.

With your next breath, let all of your tension go, paying special attention to your jaw and throat, even rubbing it a little to help relax it, and simply *be* for a moment or two, even longer if possible. Enjoy sitting and breathing deeply, empty of all thought, free of any agenda, and centered in the moment. Feel this vibration of being more aware of and connected to your intuition. Notice how peaceful, content, and even energized you feel. This is the healing force of your Spirit, and it's available to you at all times to guide you through all of life's challenges and toward its treasures. It is the real you. *Remember this.*

### Daily Ritual: Connect to the Spirit Realm

Begin tuning in to your intuition, your guiding Spirit, by centering your attention on your breathing, and then move your awareness to your heart. Relax your brow and forehead as you breathe in even more deeply, and notice how your breath is shared with all living things. Realize with your next breath that you are not and never were alone. You are deeply connected to all loving beings throughout the Universe and beyond. Breathe in slowly and deeply, and relax as you feel the subtle yet powerful stream of benevolence coming from the spirit realm to you, surrounding, supporting, guiding, serving, and loving you. Think of yourself as warm and protected as a beloved newborn swaddled in a soft blanket. Imagine that your Spirit is constantly connected to the heavenly realms of angels, guides, ancestors, nature spirits, teachers, helpers, light beings, joy guides, and other powerful holy forces unknown to you but absolutely lovingly available to assist your journey through life in every way.

Allow yourself to feel this powerful connection and let these guiding forces of love help you. Use your imagination to have a conversation with these helpers. In what areas of your life could you use the assistance of your Spirit and your spirit guides? In work? In affairs of the heart? In your creative desires? Your health? Finances? Finding your true purpose? What might you ask them through prayer, direct invocation, or a simple request? The guides are listening and are available, but you must first ask for their assistance. You must be open to guidance before these subtle forces can assist you. Once you tune in to your intuition, all sorts of wonderful guidance and assistance will start to flow toward you. That's why it is important to make it a daily habit, a regular practice, to tune in and ask for all available assistance from the subtle realms of Spirit.

### The Phone Call

A wake-up call from your Spirit and the spirit realm can be an intense, dramatic, or even life-and-death experience, such as Robert's, but it doesn't have to be. Your wake-up call can also come in more subtle yet still quite unexpected ways—even in a single moment, as it did for me.

Many years ago, when I was in my third year of college, I was living in Denver with my first serious boyfriend. We'd been together for four years and planned eventually to get married. I felt content—that is, until I received a phone call one day from my older brother, Neil, who had just graduated and was about to embark on a career with an airline. Celebrating his new status and ability to travel the world with ease, he said, "Come on, Sonia, let's go to London as soon as you can. I'll use my passes—we'll have a blast!"

Not only did his words cause me to nearly faint with excitement over such a generous invitation, but they also spoke directly to my Spirit. I felt as if I'd just come alive with all the force of a sleeping giant waking up. I was ready to see the world!

After hanging up the phone, I practically levitated to the other room to share the good news with my boyfriend. "Guess what?" I nearly gasped. "Neil just invited us to go to London with him. Isn't that fabulous?" Fully expecting him to jump for joy with me,

I was taken aback when he barely looked up from the TV, and with a genuinely confused look, asked, "Why?"

He might as well have thrown a bucket of cold water in my face, because that was so *not* the reaction I had expected. I was stunned into silence.

I remember thinking, *Why on earth would anyone ever ask <u>why</u> they should go to London?* There was no "why" involved! Who needs a reason to go to London or any other fascinating place, for that matter? Adventure, exploration, discovery—that's *why* . . . at least that explained "why" for my authentic Self, my Spirit.

Looking at each other with equal amounts of confusion, I didn't even try to explain how I felt. I could clearly see that my boyfriend didn't share my feelings. The invitation to explore the unknown didn't speak to his Spirit in the least. I had a realization in that instant, based on his one-word response, that the two of us lived in entirely different universes that would never meet. I simply shook my head at him and said, "Never mind."

Unfazed, he shrugged and said, "Okay." Then he went back to watching TV without so much as a glance back at me. Now don't get me wrong. He wasn't trying to be a jerk, nor did he lack a sense of adventure. An avid skier and bike rider, he was also a musician and sang in a band. He was in every way a loving, kind, creative guy; and I really enjoyed being with him. And yet in that moment, I realized that I'd been seriously misguided in thinking that we were two peas in a pod.

I walked back into the bedroom and sat down, still not fully believing what had just happened. More disturbing than his not wanting to go to London was the fact, which I now acknowledged to myself, that I had been planning to spend the rest of my life with the wrong person. His "Why?" instantly shattered all my illusions that we would have a happy life together. It wasn't because he didn't feel the call to travel or seek adventure. It was because the call was now so strong in me that the idea of staying in Denver and continuing on the predictable life path we were following—one which he was content to stay on—would kill my authentic Self, my Spirit.

I simply couldn't carry on. Like a wild tiger that had been unleashed and needed to run free as fast as it could, my Spirit had been fully awakened by that phone call. In a single word, I intuitively knew I needed to make drastic life changes and would. I was going to leave the relationship, leave college, leave my family, and even leave Denver so that I could follow my brother into the much bigger, exciting, exotic world that he'd just joined.

This unexpected epiphany made no rational sense at first and caught me completely off guard. Prior to this, I wasn't at all consciously aware that I felt constrained in any way. I didn't talk or dream about traveling, nor did I pine away for faraway places. I had a lot of fun in Colorado doing the same things my boyfriend did, and I wasn't unhappy or restless. It's just that in a single moment, my Spirit woke up to a brand-new vision, and when it did, I intuitively knew with every cell of my being that the world I was in and the future world I was planning (including getting married) was not for me and could not happen. Like waking up from a strange dream, I knew instantly in my heart, with absolute certainty, that everything needed to change.

Saying nothing to my boyfriend, because there was nothing really to say anyway, the next morning I submitted an application to work for an airline, as well. The timing was perfect, and I was interviewed and hired within a week. I had exactly three days to pack my bags and move to Kansas City for training, which meant that I had to quit school, break up with my boyfriend, and move out in that brief time frame if I intended to follow through on all this.

My intellect and emotions were going crazy. *Why am I doing this? How can I be so cruel to break up with my boyfriend and leave just like that? I haven't even finished college! How can I leave Denver? What will I say to my parents? This makes no logical sense.* I continued to chastise myself. I couldn't explain my decision nor could I justify or rationalize it. And I certainly couldn't feel guilt-free about it . . . yet I couldn't stop it either. Every fiber in my body was marching forward, never for one second hesitating or questioning my intuition as to whether this was absolutely correct for me to do. So I followed my heart and was gone three days later.

Needless to say, the ending at home didn't go well. My boyfriend was stunned, hurt, horrified, and angry. But one day, after he screamed at me yet again for abandoning him, I quietly asked him, in all sincerity, "Do you really feel, in your heart, that this is the wrong thing for me to do?"

My question quieted him, and he didn't speak for what seemed like forever. Then he looked at me with sadness, and said, "No, I don't. Doing what you're doing and leaving is the right thing for you. I'm going nowhere but you're going places, and I know it. It would have happened sooner or later. I'm just sad it was sooner."

I wish I could say that my wake-up call instantly led to a brilliant life and I lived happily ever after, but it didn't unfold quite that way. Following my intuition and leaving my home, school, family, and boyfriend in such an impulsive manner rocked my world. Or more accurately, it totally shattered it. I went through all kinds of emotional and even physical confusion, upheaval, and pain in the following months. I had to let my entire identity go and discover a whole new one. After my training in Kansas City, I ended up being based in Chicago, which was utterly intimidating, as was flying all over the country. I was lonely and insecure, but I never, ever once felt that I'd made a mistake. As difficult as following my intuition and my Spirit was, it was something that I couldn't ignore.

That's how a powerful wake-up call from Spirit works. It pulls, prods, and pushes you to be honest with yourself, to remember your soul intentions, to face your greatest fears, to let go of what isn't working or in alignment with your soul and reach for your fullest potential. It moves you in the direction of your most authentic Self and urges you to commence your soul's plan. No matter where you are in life, if the direction you're pointing is not in alignment with your soul's intentions, your intuition—the pulse of your Spirit—will let you know. A wake-up call is not always about bringing you comfort and ease; it's about furthering your soul's growth, developing your authentic Self, and strengthening your connection to your true and Divine nature. It's about transformation from fear and control to heart and truth, from human to Divine Self, which is highly demanding and can be frightening at times. The only thing more frightening, however, is not following your intuition, not trusting your Spirit, and remaining disconnected from who you really are, stuck in a life of no genuine meaning or purpose.

In my case, my ultimate purpose wasn't working for an airline. In fact, that job merely served as a stepping-stone to other highly transformational experiences that followed. Yet my soul's growth trajectory made it necessary for me to begin in that way in order to access new opportunities. The force of intuition within me didn't stop with the phone call from my brother that day. It *began* that day. It even pushed me to take a leave of absence from my airline job several times as quickly as it had persuaded me to apply for it, so that I could carry on with my soul's plan. In the same crazy fashion, it urged me to move to Paris and finish school there, then head back to Chicago. Eventually, my Spirit, through my intuition, led me to start on the path of teaching and writing, which at first seemed as irrational and risky as my initial move from Denver. Nevertheless, I followed.

Each intuitive push taught me more soul lessons and developed within me the courage necessary to fulfill my soul's mission. My Spirit continues to guide me today. It continues to shake my foundation, rock my boat, scare my ego, and reward me beyond my wildest dreams. I've simply learned to recognize it and trust in its power without question.

### Tuning In

Whether the call from your Spirit comes in subtle intuitive prods or radical "come to Jesus" moments of life and death (or both), the key is to know that these urges from your authentic Self will continue to appear, over and over again, throughout your entire life, always leading you home to your Divine nature.

The key is to recognize a wake-up call from your Spirit and be open to following it, even if not immediately. To do so is to recognize your authentic power rising from within and allow it to move you in the direction of your most holy and authentic Self and your true soul plan and purpose. Be prepared for your thinking mind, and those of others, to resist, fight back, and even try to dismiss or demean your efforts to follow your truth. Remember that the ego is uncomfortable with and resistant to change, and your loved ones may be reacting out of the fear that they're losing you.

Remind yourself and those around you that the only part of you they will lose is the part that doesn't reflect or align with your true Self. Avoid the temptation to seek the opinions or approval of others before you listen. This will only confuse you and make you feel crazy, as some might urge you on while others try to scare you away from your heart.

To be empowered means to follow your own heart, even if doing so is uncomfortable, disruptive, unpopular, or can't be explained to others right now, or ever. Your intuition can be trusted, as it is there to keep you true to your authentic Self, if you listen. Know that you have great support and assistance available to you at all times in the subtle realms, and you're being watched over and loved every step of the way as you follow your inner light. Use your breathing techniques to calm your uncertain and fearful mind and fully tune in to your opening heart, and you will feel this holy escort surrounding you no matter what choices and changes you must make.

### Asking the Questions

Close your eyes and calmly breathe in and out through your nose. Start with a sigh or two to help you relax. Massage your jaw and throat a little to release even more tension and fear held in that part of your body, your expression center. Feel the energetic tension that your racing mind creates in your body. Do you notice the way in which it drains your energy, your life force, your kefi, right out of you?

Now relax the tension in your neck and throat as much as possible with a few gentle stretches and take in a deep, easy, belly-filling breath. Don't force your breath to enter your body by raising your shoulders and holding your head back. Rather, keep your shoulders comfortably relaxed and down, and allow your belly to pull the air in naturally without any tension at all. Exhale by releasing the sound "Ah," and then bring the corners of your lips up to your ears in a gentle smile.

Next, take out your journal and tune inward. Contemplate each of the following questions and invite your intuition, your Divine Spirit, your most authentic Self, to respond to each one, preferably out loud, before writing your answer down. Give yourself plenty of time to feel the genuine response coming from your heart, the source of your power.

- What subtle intuitive signals do you feel calling you back to your authentic Self?

- Where might you be perpetuating something in your life that doesn't feel fully in alignment with your Spirit?

- Are you trying to "make the shoe fit" in a relationship, job, living arrangement, or other circumstance, even though you intuitively know that your Spirit is not at all in alignment with the situation?

- Where do you feel numb, uninspired, or even trapped in life?

- Have you received a message from Spirit in the form of a conversation or other unexpected communication that has caught your attention, opened up a possibility that you hadn't considered before, or revealed an avenue that greatly appeals to you, even though it may make no logical sense or seem impossible to pursue?

- What would your heart love to do that your head (or other people) says is not possible?

- Are you connected to people who stifle your Spirit? Who are they? In what way does their behavior or energy not feel right or supportive to you?

After writing down your answers, set aside your journal and remain seated. Close your eyes, and calmly breathe in and out through your nose. Start with a sigh or two to help you relax. Notice any energetic release or shift you may feel as a result of openly acknowledging, without resistance, the intuitive call of your Spirit. Feel that distinct vibration coursing through your body and how different it feels from focusing on your intellect alone.

You may discover, as I did, that the course you are presently on is not in alignment with your true Spirit. This may come as a complete surprise or may merely bring to light what you'd been keeping in the recesses of your mind for some time. Your wake-up call makes you aware of discrepancies between the path you are on and your soul purpose, and invites you to correct your course. While this can be highly destabilizing to your present life, know that your intuition will eventually lead you back to your most authentic Self if you tune in and follow the call. Any other existence would be unfulfilling and uninspiring. Notice what you discover when you trust your intuition to guide you every step of the way, even if it does seem frightening at times.

With your next breath, let all of your tension go and simply *be* for a moment or two, even longer if possible. Enjoy sitting and breathing deeply, empty of all thought, free of any agenda, centered in the moment. Feel this vibration of being connected to Spirit. Notice how peaceful, content, and even energized you feel. Feel the loving power of your guiding Spirit, and know it's available to you at all times. It is the real you. *Remember this.*

### *Daily Ritual: Breathe to Set Good Boundaries*

Learn to pause and take a breath before you speak or act. Take two or three breaths, if possible. Focus your full attention on your heart and your inner guidance as you breathe before engaging with the world. One way to remind yourself to do so is to put a rubber band around your wrist and gently snap it from time to time. The physical stimulation will reinforce in your mind that it's important to breathe before you act. Breathing deeply and calmly allows you to respond and create from the heart and your true Self; life without breath causes you to react from your head and leaves you feeling controlled, controlling, overwhelmed, and powerless.

As you breathe, pay attention to your heart rate. If it seems fast, your body might be in a fight-or-flight state. If so, continue breathing and give yourself permission to relax and proceed slowly without being rushed. Don't force an action until you feel grounded and your body is aligned with your Spirit. Each breath pulls your Spirit more fully into your body and allows you to get centered in your authentic Self. As easy as it might be to skip practicing this regularly, remember that breathing mindfully gives you the power to set up healthy boundaries for yourself, an essential part of living an intuitively guided life. As you connect with your Spirit, ask it to take charge and relieve your mind of all duties. Tell your intellect that your Spirit is there to guide and protect you, so now you can fully relax. You are safe.

Now let's take it a step further. Empowered by your intuition and your connection to your Spirit, decide with your next breath that you will *not* say yes when you really mean no (and vice versa) when dealing with requests from other people. It's also okay not to answer until you have a chance to breathe deeply and consult with your intuition, your Spirit, to help you discover what your true response is. To make that happen, all you have to say is: "I need a few minutes to think about it."

If you feel pressured by someone to respond before you connect with your breath and consult with your intuition, then step away for a moment. For example, briefly excuse yourself to go to the restroom or to go outside for some air. Once you're out of the situation, relax and breathe. Tuning in to your intuition need not be difficult—in fact, it's the opposite of difficult. It simply requires a moment of inward reflection, a little space, and a few deep, slow breaths. Take these steps and you will succeed.

Don't be afraid to set up healthy boundaries that give you the space you need to tune in to your inner voice and speak the truth of your Spirit, and don't be afraid to speak up and share those boundaries with others. A truthful response (even if it's a refusal) is surprisingly powerful and respected. What you say may be challenged, but resist the temptation to become defensive. Breathe and be silent instead. By doing so, you'll maintain your connection to Spirit and others will feel it. If necessary, simply repeat your response with love and respect.

Remember that you don't need to look far to tune in to the guiding power of your Spirit. Your breath allows you to connect to it. Each day, make a conscious effort to focus on your breathing, for it is the key that unlocks the door to your deepest wisdom and truth.

## The Pilgrimage

At times our Spirit wakes us up with a start. At other times, we know we're asleep to our Spirit and so go in search of how to wake up. It's just important to look in the right place.

Patrick was an adventure traveler, an interested observer of the human race, of all things different and unusual. His Spirit was happiest when he was packing his bags and preparing for some far-off destination—the more exotic, the better. He had traveled a lot in his life, especially when he was younger, and he loved every minute of it—even the moments when he was extremely uncomfortable. Comfort didn't really matter to him. An adventure was an adventure, and that's when he felt the most alive and vital.

Patrick never used to think twice about dropping everything to get on a bicycle, bus, train, or airplane and head off into the unknown. He loved it, in fact. Learning something new directly from experience was as good as life could get. He fondly recalled his most amazing experiences, such as the time he was in China and saw people eating monkey brains directly from their crushed skulls. He was simultaneously grossed out and fascinated. *People really do that?*

Once when he was in Tokyo, he visited a public steam bath. After a wonderfully relaxing few hours, he stood up to leave only to realize that he was so tall that he could see directly over the wall separating the men's bath from the women's. There he discovered a room full of beautiful naked women lounging around, some combing each other's hair. That was a bath he never forgot! On another occasion, he was riding a horse across an open field in France, when he rode right through the most spectacular cloud of turquoise butterflies that was so thick he couldn't see a foot in front of him.

He never would have truly understood the meaning of those events by reading about them in a book. He firmly believed that a person had to be there, in the flesh, to feel the effect of such vivid experiences. That is why he wandered so fearlessly into the unknown. It kept him very much in the present moment.

As he got older, however, Patrick became more "responsible" and less carefree. He got married, bought a house, and started a family. He found himself becoming surprisingly more cautious, even resistant, when it came to taking off on big adventures. Even though he had his own business and could go whenever he wanted to, he worried that he might lose clients, or that something would go wrong while he was away and he'd regret being gone. He believed he had too much to lose, so he felt as if he couldn't travel as often or as far. It's not that he didn't long for big adventures. He did. He just didn't let himself be moved enough to act on his inner yearnings.

This didn't benefit him or help him stay connected to his Spirit. Getting caught up in his day-to-day life—sitting at his desk for several hours, typing away on his computer, talking on the phone—cut him off completely from his intuition—his inner teacher and guide—and caused him to become increasingly irritable, negative, critical, and judgmental. This negatively affected the people closest to him, but he was especially hard on himself. He no longer saw the wonder in life. He only saw "duty" and resented it.

In spite of this, what he did create was a happy family who loved him very much and could see and feel his Spirit languishing as his thoughts crushed him. It wasn't easy to watch or experience this, and it actually frustrated them, as well. Finally, as a means to help Patrick reconnect to his inner guide, his wife hatched a plan to send him on the biggest adventure she could conceive of: a trek to Mount Kailash in the Tibetan Himalayas, considered by many ancient religions, including the Hindus and Buddhists, to be the holiest place on Earth and the ultimate spiritual pilgrimage a person can make.

If that didn't resuscitate his dormant Spirit and reconnect him to his inner guidance, nothing would. Patrick's family presented this gift to him on Christmas, and he was to leave the following August, giving him plenty of time to prepare for his absence from his business as well as get into shape for the rigorous hike ahead. He had no excuse to say no or put it off.

Patrick was speechless and completely surprised. He didn't know what to say. It was just what he needed to revive himself, he thought, and he knew he had his family's support, so his only choice was to trust this gesture. He gratefully accepted the gift and immediately got excited. Since it was known to be an arduous trip to the nearly 22,000-foot summit (with a high probability of bad weather to boot), he had a big challenge in front of him and was thrilled by it. It felt good to get ready for adventure. It felt right.

The idea of the trip kept him charged for months, and he told everyone he was going. It wowed them. Tibet sounded so exotic and dangerous, but most of all, it seemed so *spiritual*. Once he started on his journey, the reality of his experience was quite different from the fantasies he had carried about it, however. For one thing, he was traveling with a motley crew, or so he judged at first. They just didn't seem that spiritual, although he had to admit that he didn't appear to be that spiritual either. His primary guide was one of the world's foremost Tibetan scholars, and his partner was a filmmaker. They seemed interesting enough, if a little dry and subdued. The other pilgrims, of whom there were only three, were as different from him as he could imagine. One was an English countess, another a Scottish teacher, and the third a researcher and philosopher from Oregon. *Okay,* he thought, once all the introductions were made, *let the adventure begin!*

They quickly bonded, mostly over the challenging conditions they faced on the mountain, along with the bare minimum of comforts they were given to share once they set out. The mountain path was formidable: jagged, rocky terrain covered in snow, often with water running underneath it. The weather was even worse. The temperatures were well below freezing, while constant stiff winds blew harshly from the north, bringing along with them an unending flurry of wet, freezing snow and rain.

The pilgrimage consisted of walking 52 miles (half of them uphill) at an incredibly slow, grueling pace. To make matters worse, Patrick noted that most of his group clearly didn't read the memo about getting in shape for their trek and had a very hard time trying to keep up. And of course, everyone was affected by the altitude, which made breathing difficult. Patrick felt as if he'd pass out at any given moment. The highlight at the end of each day was getting to camp and resting. They stayed in small yurts and ate yak (and more yak) for all of their meals. (This is a particularly strong, tough meat that most of the country's inhabitants subsist on.) It wasn't something to write home about—that was for certain.

Day after day, Patrick's patience worsened, along with the weather conditions on the mountain. The rest of the crew members were clearly struggling with the altitude, and they were going even slower than the already unbearable pace they had set in the beginning. Patrick thought for sure he was going to catch frostbite if he didn't move faster. Finally, he couldn't take it anymore. He broke free from the group and walked ahead, telling them that he'd meet them at the campsite they were all headed to.

As he started to find his own pace, he began to reflect on what a miserable situation he found himself in. He wasn't having fun, and it certainly wasn't glamorous. It didn't even feel spiritual! It was just hard work in miserable conditions with people who challenged his patience. To make matters worse, the fog and clouds were so low that even though he was on the most sacred mountain in the world, he couldn't see it. He couldn't help but mutter to himself: *Thanks a lot for the gift. What on earth did I ever do to deserve a punishment like this?!*

As he walked, he became a bit disoriented in the fog and falling snow. He was so cold he worried that he would freeze to death. He longed to be home, in his bed, in the comfort of the wonderful life he had there. Oh, the irony! When he was there, he thought it lacked genuine meaning, but now, with each labored breath he drew in, his home seemed to be the holiest place on Earth. And he missed his family. He came here to receive some kind of spiritual insight, and instead, he was pretty sure that all he would receive was a bad case of hypothermia.

*Is this all there is?* he wondered as he inched forward. He wasn't able to let his thoughts float toward spiritual matters. He had to focus on surviving until he got to the next camp, wherever that was. And since he'd been walking for hours, he began to worry about that, too. He should have been there by now.

It was getting later and colder, and he started to think about how he had expected this pilgrimage to somehow make him wiser and more spiritual. He surely wasn't feeling either in the moment. All he could feel was fear, not only because he thought he was going to freeze to death or keel over from altitude sickness (as indicated by the splitting headache he had and the fact the he could barely breathe), but also because a new fear was sneaking in and taking over. He was terrified that he was lost. In fact, he was sure of it.

A new wave of anxiety passed through his nervous system, and he didn't know whether to be angry, pray, turn around, sit down, start running, or laugh out loud. Since the decision was too great to make, he just kept walking straight ahead into the blustering wind.

Eventually his brain froze, or at least he assumed it did because he stopped being afraid. In fact, he stopped thinking altogether and just walked. Almost immediately, things got easier. The outer conditions didn't change; he just stopped fighting against them. It was what it was. He accepted that and settled down and relaxed. *Just keep putting one foot in front of the other,* he told himself. *It has to lead somewhere.* As he continued hiking, breathing the best he could, a miraculous thing happened. He started to feel the Spirit of the mountain, and it was as magnificent as he was told. He couldn't see it, but he felt its power under his feet. It was alive and breathing. He calmed down even more and began to listen to the mountain as he walked.

No longer absorbed in his own mental struggles, he became quite aware and alert. He could intuitively feel the Spirit of the blowing north wind. It challenged him to be mindful of where he was going. Soaking wet, he could feel the Spirit of the rain and snow washing off his pitiful attempts to control everything. He could even feel the spirits of the hundreds of thousands of pilgrims who had trekked this same mountain, this very same path before him for thousands of years. His fear lifted, and his mind felt clear and strong.

He continued on for a few short minutes when he saw another pilgrim with his wife and baby in the not-too-far distance. They had stopped and were huddled together. He noticed the pilgrim because he was wearing a brilliant turquoise quilted jacket, and it almost seemed to sparkle against the gray-white backdrop of the mountain. He approached the family and smiled. The man nodded but didn't smile back, and his wife looked at Patrick curiously but didn't reveal anything else. She cuddled her baby, bundled up and bound tightly to her in a sling, and Patrick marveled that she and the child—in fact, all three of them—seemed so calm and serene in such harsh conditions.

Patrick motioned in an attempt to ask if he could sit with them for a while. They nodded and seemed to give off a welcoming energy. They couldn't communicate, as they didn't speak each other's language, so they just sat together in silence. Patrick was glad not to be alone. He could tell by their clothing that they were nomads, people who roamed the lands with their tribe. The man was young, maybe 25 or so, but the lines on his face were already deeply carved, revealing years of surviving harsh living conditions. But the bright sparkle of his eyes made him seem eternally youthful. His wife looked like a teenager, and although he couldn't see the baby fully, he guessed that the little one was just a few months old.

As they sat together, Patrick remembered that he had a dried-yak sandwich in his backpack. Wanting to give them a gift for their kindness, he pulled it out and offered to share it with them. They accepted graciously, and the three of them sat eating their small pieces. After a few minutes, the cold winds kicked in once again, and they all stood up to resume their journey.

As they walked, the man began to sing a lovely song. His voice was so clear and pure it moved Patrick to his very core. After a few moments, the wife also began to sing, again with a stunningly clear voice that gave a glimpse of her beautiful open heart and sweet Spirit. Not wanting to be left out, Patrick burst into his personal rendition of "I've Been Working on the Railroad" and sang every verse as the pilgrims smiled brightly.

After the impromptu concert, they continued to walk the path in silence, and a thought struck Patrick like a lightning bolt. *This is the gift I'm supposed to receive from my pilgrimage. It's not the mountain, this place, or even the adventure of travel like I thought it would be. It's simply being present, heart-to-heart, with other human beings.*

His heart fully expanded, his mind absolutely calm, Patrick was awed by his realization. He took a deep breath and smiled. "What better gift could I ever receive than this?"

Just then, his new friend reached inside his turquoise jacket and pulled out a tiny banana-shaped children's sucker. It had goofy eyes and a silly smile, and looked like it had seen a million miles of trekking in that nomad's possession. The man gazed at it for a moment as if saying good-bye and then handed it to Patrick.

It was so ridiculous that it made Patrick laugh out loud. This is what he came to Mount Kailash for: this silly little smiling sucker! It summed up the entire experience better than words ever could.

Patrick made it to the camp about 45 minutes later, and the pilgrims continued on their way. For the first time since his great journey began, he slept soundly. Three weeks later, he returned to his family and regular life . . . but he wasn't the same man who had left a month earlier. He no longer believed that he needed to do something grand or dramatic in order to live his Spirit. He simply had to listen to his heart and inner guidance, embrace whatever was in front of him with his whole heart—instead of fighting it—and connect with a smile, a song if possible, and a sucker.

### Tuning In

The wake-up call to follow your intuition isn't necessarily a grand to-do. Rather, it can be a subtle, yet powerful, inner experience. You don't have to undergo some earth-shattering experience to make a positive connection, although your ego will certainly try to make you believe that this is necessary. In fact, it will try to convince you that making the shift to living a Spirit-guided life is extraordinarily complicated, difficult, and unreasonable. Remember that your ego will do anything to stay in control.

Living an intuitively guided life is really about shifting your perception. When you stop looking at the world with such a limited view, believing that what you see in front of you at the moment is all there is, and choose instead to look from your heart, recognizing and appreciating there is always more in the unseen, yet-to-be-revealed world, your personal connection to your Spirit and all of your Divine helpers is in place.

### Asking the Questions

Close your eyes and calmly breathe in and out through your nose. Start with a sigh or two to help you relax. Massage your jaw and throat a little to release even more tension and fear held in that part of your body, your expression center. Feel the energetic tension that your racing mind creates in your body. Do you notice how it drains your energy, your life force, your kefi, right out of you?

Now relax the tension in your neck and throat as much as possible with a few gentle stretches and take in a deep, easy, belly-filling breath. Don't force your breath to enter your body by raising your shoulders and holding your head back. Rather, keep your shoulders comfortably relaxed and down, and allow your belly to pull the air in naturally without any tension at all. Exhale by releasing the sound "Ah," and then bring the corners of your lips up to your ears in a gentle smile.

Next, take out your journal and tune inward. Contemplate each of the following questions, and allow your intuition, your most authentic Self, to respond to each one. Breathe deeply and give yourself plenty of time to tune in to the genuine response coming from your heart.

- What are you most seeking, searching, or yearning for these days? Can you put it into words? Do you feel like something is missing? What are your heartfelt longings? Do you know?

- Are you resigned to ignoring or living with any soul void, or do you feel compelled to pay attention to it?

- Where might you discover what you're looking for? Have you thought about it?

- Have you verbally acknowledged any of your deeper inner yearnings to anyone, or have you tended to keep them to yourself? Where do you think these messages come from?

- Are you afraid your inner yearnings, if acted upon, might be too disruptive to your life to admit? What might be most challenged?

- How do you spend your free time?

- What responsibilities are you now carrying? Do you feel overwhelmed by them, or are they manageable?

- Do you ever wonder if you're a drag? In other words, do people ever suggest that you take away their fun, leave them feeling drained, or are a real "downer"? Are you? What might be the real reason you aren't filled with more joy? What might you do about it?

- Are you held down by someone you might call a "drag" on your Spirit? What is your relationship? Are you able to consider making a change or moving away from that person?

- Do you feel connected to spontaneous joy most of the time? Sometimes? Rarely? Never? How might you connect with more joy?

- What do you struggle with most: external conditions or internal ones?

- Do you allow your intuition—your guiding Spirit— to influence your life, or do you tend to block it or ignore it?

After writing down your answers, set aside your journal and remain seated. Close your eyes, and calmly breathe in and out through your nose. Start with releasing a sigh or two to help you relax. Reflect on the vibration you send to others, and the effect their vibration has on you. Notice the distinct energetic differences between the vibration of ego (heavy, tense, contracted) and the vibration of your inner guiding Spirit (light, calm, expansive).

With your next breath, let all of your tension go and simply *be* for a moment or two, even longer if possible. Enjoy sitting and breathing deeply, empty of all thought, free of any agenda, centered in the moment. Feel this vibration of being connected to your inner knowing. Notice how peaceful, content, and even energized you feel. This is the power of your intuition—your Spirit—and it's available to you at all times. It is the real you. *Remember this.*

### Daily Ritual: Notice the Light of Spirit in Your Eyes

First thing in the morning and before retiring at night, stand before a mirror and look yourself directly in the eyes. Do you have a sparkle in your eyes? Can you see the light? If not, put the corners of your lips up to your ears and smile, and watch it appear. Keep trying until you see the light. This powerful light is the messenger that carries inner guidance from your heart to your mind, where it can help you make better, more authentic, more loving decisions that resonate with your true Self. It is the same light of Spirit you see in others—equally beautiful in all.

Once you start recognizing this inner light in everyone you meet, your life will quickly and profoundly shift. Synchronicities will overflow. Doors will swing open. Opportunities will fly at you. As you activate your inner eye and let it light your way, the world around you dramatically changes for the better. You will start to intuitively "see" more deeply into situations and people. You'll intuitively see what your intellectual mind missed. You'll also begin to see that in every situation there is an opportunity to advance, succeed, and find support and assistance, if only you look deeply enough.

✳

Once we are called to wake up to our Spirit, our perspectives and priorities begin to radically shift. What once felt so important is now less so. What once felt oppressive and confining starts to evaporate and open up, if not disappear altogether. And what we once thought of the world—and most of all, ourselves—begins to shift and expand in more optimistic, promising, and exciting ways. Once we answer the sweet calling of our Spirit and open up to our inner guidance, we begin to relax and start to live. We begin to experience freedom from our anxieties and fears and cannot help but follow the magnetic pull of inner guidance.

Now that we've awakened to the presence and power of our guiding Spirit, we're ready to move into the second step: *Digging Deep.* Let's go to the next chapter and continue the journey to living a more authentic, empowered life.

✳ ✳ ✳

# Chapter Three

# STEP TWO: DIGGING DEEP

The second step in following our intuition is fueled by curiosity. We usually enter this step when we've experienced some type of wake-up call, yet we still feel hesitant to trust our intuition. We need more evidence that we can rely on what we feel in our heart before we make such a big change in our life. Even though we aren't happy or satisfied with the way things are, we still need to be convinced that making the shift to tune in to our heart and follow our Spirit is a safe and sound alternative. And so, we start to *dig deeper* for proof that intuition is real and something we can depend upon. This step often represents the beginning of a lengthy inner struggle because, as we start to tune in to our Spirit and follow our intuition (the third step), our ego can be counted on to put up a good deal of resistance. In some cases, it's a battle that never ends.

During this step, we usually become avid and eager students, looking for evidence that intuition isn't some crazy thing to dismiss or laugh off. We look for others who are openly following their intuition and having good results. We seek authorities we can trust who will validate intuition as reliable and give us the "go ahead" to listen to our hearts and tell us it's okay, for example, to pick out titles from the spiritual section of bookstores, attend local spiritual seminars, or subscribe to online programs hosted by experts. We listen for and engage in discussions about intuition and Spirit with like-minded people. And with the enthusiasm of pursuing a new hobby, we often dive into our discovery process with gusto, hopeful that we're finally on the path to feeling better in our own skin. Once we begin our search, we inevitably dig up exciting, encouraging evidence and meet kindred spirits, all convincing us that we should indeed trust our "vibes." And yet, even with all of that encouragement and good company, often a part of us still lingers that doubts and hesitates to fully trust, let alone follow, our inner guidance and change the way we live our lives.

The Digging Deep step, like falling in love, is exciting and intoxicating. It's as if a giant curtain has been pulled back and we're allowed to witness the profound inner workings of our true Self. This step is an important one and serves as a stepping-stone to taking the leap necessary to fully surrender to our inner guidance. The more evidence and testimonials we gather about the legitimacy of intuition and the power of living our Spirit, the more inclined to listen to and trust our inner voice we become. It is, after all, a big decision—and a life changing one, because once made there is no going back. So, naturally, we proceed with great caution.

As we start to dig deeper for reasons to trust our intuition, it's almost as though the Universe starts to flirt with us, teasing us with its own subtle affirmations that we are indeed on the right track, some of which may quite seem magical. Poignant insights jump out of nowhere. Synchronistic experiences seem to just fall in our lap. A book might jump off a shelf and into our hands in the bookstore, for instance, or we may coincidentally overhear an enlightening conversation on a subject with which we are struggling, and be drawn in. We might turn on the radio at the precise moment to hear a relevant interview with an influential spiritual teacher we hadn't heard of before. We may have a huge insight as though our Spirit is speaking directly to us while receiving a healing massage or during a quiet yoga class. We may even be sitting at the beach, in awe of our beautiful surroundings, when we spontaneously have an "Aha!" moment. We might spontaneously know exactly what to do for our dying mother or come up with the perfect solution for a nagging problem we've been long struggling with just as we wake up in the morning. We might receive something in the mail inviting us to a retreat just when we're on the verge of emotional collapse, or meet someone in line at the local coffee shop who, in casual conversation, makes us aware of an opportunity that we've been searching for to no avail.

We can't deny it. This Universe suddenly seems to be speaking to us from every direction in so many ways we never were aware of before. We can't help but notice all the signals our Spirit and heavenly helpers are sending our way each and every moment of the day. Once we start digging deeper and asking for affirmation from our Spirit that tuning in is worthwhile, we'll be amazed by how often these Divine assists suddenly come our way. Like confetti falling from the sky, they are everywhere.

And yet, while digging deeper and learning all you can about your intuition is an important step in returning to Self, it is also important to realize that there's a big difference between learning *about* something and learning via firsthand *experience.* Your intellect alone can't empower your life. At best it serves to connect you with your true inner power, and, at worst, it stands in the way. It isn't enough simply to be aware of your intuition, as if watching on the sidelines. You can only truly know the power of your guiding Spirit when you make direct contact with your intuition and act on its guidance.

What helps while digging for evidence that you *can* safely trust your Spirit to guide you is to make it a daily practice to verbally express what you intuitively feel, *out loud as soon as you feel it,* so you can't deny what your intuition is saying. By developing the habit of openly expressing what your intuition is sharing with you, you can't ignore its empowering guidance. For example, you might say, out loud, "My gut tells me this is a good project to pursue," even though you aren't sure others will believe it. Or you might say, out loud, "My vibes tell me that the man who wants to date me is a good guy and someone I should consider." Or while in the car you may say, "I have a gut feeling this isn't the correct way to go," when taking a new route to an unknown restaurant.

The very act of speaking these things out loud allows you to hear the sound of your own voice and check in with whether or not what your inner voice is saying resonates in your body. If it does resonate, it will be surprisingly easy to follow it. If it doesn't, you can ask yourself what is "off" about your intuitive feeling. Doing this exercise, out loud and whenever possible (and I believe it is always possible), is much like turning on a rusty faucet and letting the water run until it becomes clear. The more you articulate your intuitive feelings, the clearer they become.

### Fear of Commitment

While it's an important first step to wake up to the call of Spirit within, unless you dig deeper to connect with your Spirit you'll experience little change. The challenge is to respond to the call back to inner truth and guidance by digging deeply enough into yourself to find center—not simply going through the motions but not doing the real work, believing this is enough. You have no one to fool but yourself, and the loss will be your own. How satisfied you feel in life accurately reflects how deeply you are truly digging. I have many students and clients who are great enthusiasts for tuning inward when in my classroom or consulting room, but once they leave they often leave their efforts behind, as well. And this brings them no closer to a true sense of self or purpose and keeps them as out of touch with their intuition and Spirit as if they hadn't woken up at all.

Philip, a consultant working with a large firm in Missouri, whose true love was landscaping and gardening, had been a student of mine for several years. He was drawn to me because he was interested in learning how to live a more authentic, intuitively guided life and thought I could help him succeed. Together we focused on his biggest challenge, which mainly consisted of his feeling dissatisfied with his job, although he was very good at it and made a good living. He wanted to find his inner voice to help him feel more purposeful and peaceful with the way his life was going. He was particularly interested in ways in which he could make specific shifts to better align himself with his intuition so he might either find his true calling and make a change or begin to feel better about the life he had now and settle down.

In the beginning of our work together, he was very excited and wanted to learn all he could as fast as he could. He seemed to genuinely enjoy the process of discovering more about his intuition and agreed with me on the many reasons he should dig deep within to listen to it. He sensed the power that comes from following intuition over merely thinking about it, and greatly wanted to experience this for himself. In support of his desire I sent him off with a list of tools and practices (most of which are in this book) to keep him tuned in on his own, as well as a list of books to read both to help open and quiet his mind and also to put to rest the endless questions he felt he needed to have answered before he felt he could fully trust his inner guidance. He loved the material I suggested and said he carried the books with him everywhere he went.

The next step in following his intuition was more involved and took an even greater effort on his part. I invited Philip to support his intention by enrolling in some courses where he could practice tuning in to his intuition under the direction of a mentor, in a safe setting where taking risks would hold no dire consequences. Some of the classes I recommended were geared toward strengthening his intuition, but others were more directly related to exploring his heart's true desire, which was in landscape design, something his intuition clearly reminded him that he loved but had never allowed himself to pursue.

Although hesitant to commit his time, he found these suggestions doable. The courses on intuition were often only one day in length or during a weekend, so he could easily fit them into his schedule without disruption, and he loved them. The nearby community college even offered classes in landscape design one night a week, so he didn't have any trouble making time for them either.

When we touched base a few months after the first of these classes ended, Philip expressed a desire to dig even deeper. This time I suggested he commit to a daily practice consisting of gentle breathing to center himself on his heart, and ten minutes of meditation to help him tune inward and listen, all of which would take no more than 15 minutes, followed by expressing out loud any insights or guidance that might come to him throughout the day. He was eager to get started, and we parted with his commitment not only to go inward but also to anchor his day-to-day life by tuning in regularly and acknowledging his guidance, with these practices to support him.

We spoke again six months later, and the minute I heard his voice I could tell he was unsettled and frustrated, and had fallen off track with his Spirit. His job as a consultant was going well enough, but he wasn't 100 percent confident that he could trust the people he worked for. At the same time, a former client wanted to hire him as an employee, and a good friend was proposing that they form a consulting partnership together. With all of these options dancing before his eyes, he'd lost touch with his intuition and was very confused.

Before I suggested anything, I asked Philip if he had been making the effort to tap into his own intuition on these questions through the daily practices I'd suggested.

He paused and then said, "Well, I fully intended to. It's just that this is my busiest time of the year, and I can't commit to anything right now."

I didn't respond right away so that he could hear his own words resonate in the world. "So," I eventually replied, "just to make sure I understand, you can't seem to get clear guidance from your Spirit, and yet you can't tune in to your intuition for a few minutes a day because it's not convenient. Although you want to experience the guidance and power of your Spirit, you don't have time to tune in because other things are more important at the moment. Is that right?"

Philip burst out laughing. "Yes, I guess that's exactly what I just said! I can't believe I said it, but it's true." He was genuinely surprised to see his resistance so clearly mirrored back to him.

"I had no idea until this moment just how much I was avoiding doing this work. Wow! What a shock! Why is that?"

It was a good question, and one we must all ask ourselves. Wanting, even intending to listen to Spirit and follow our intuition is quite different from actually tuning in to it on a daily basis. Philip's resistance, perhaps every person's resistance, lies in the fact that with inner guidance usually comes the suggestion to make a significant change from the way we are presently doing things, and we may not be prepared or willing to do that.

I actually believe the biggest reason we don't listen to our intuition is because it usually guides us to make often highly disruptive changes to the ways things are, and we're afraid of or averse to facing that disruption. It is the proverbial case of wanting our cake and eating it, too. We want to be guided by our intuition, unless of course it asks us to do something that feels threatening or could make us uncomfortable. Because of our fear and resistance to change, we stop ourselves from making the empowering decision to commit to a regular practice. Admitting that we may need to make significant changes in life in order to be happier and more in alignment with our Spirit can be difficult, even threatening.

In Philip's case, on the surface he avoided listening to his intuition because his rational mind persuaded him that it would be a waste of his precious time and he was too busy anyway. But underneath those superficial rationalizations, he and I quickly uncovered something deeper. By actively tuning in to his inner guidance, he might have to face the deeper truth that he didn't want his job as a consultant and would much rather become a full-time landscape gardener. This scared him.

Landscape gardening wasn't financially sound, or so he thought. How could he pay his rent? A cascading litany of concerns clouded his thinking. He feared that acknowledging his intuition and its underlying messages would be like letting the genie out of the bottle, causing him to make changes he couldn't afford.

It would be too expensive, impractical, and unreliable, he feared, so he avoided it altogether. He blamed his busy life, but in fact, he made his life too busy so he wouldn't have to listen to his Spirit's guidance. The idea that openly expressing his intuition would be destabilizing and financially ruinous made it easier for him to tune it out, and with it his authentic Self.

As with Philip, fear is the number one obstacle to tuning in to intuition I encounter with my clients all over the world. While we want to transform into more spiritual beings and lead our lives by the guiding wisdom and truth of our hearts, we fear the effort may be too complicated and the rewards not guaranteed. So we go far enough to show interest, but stop short of allowing ourselves to explore our intuition in the most direct way—because this is where "the rubber meets the road."

In acknowledging our intuition we most likely have to face making real changes that may feel too risky to consider. The paradox is that in voicing our intuition regularly we begin to build the confidence and inner strength needed to make the changes our Spirit is calling for without resistance and fear. At the same time, we come to realize at the deepest level that the risks we fear are more likely risks to our sense of control than to our safety. The more we announce our intuition, the easier it becomes to trust it. And with following the suggestions we intuitively receive to change our lives also comes the ways in which we can successfully do so. Intuition guides us as we go, much like the headlights of a car do on a dark road at night. It lights up the way right before us, and while sometimes we can't see much beyond that, following the light is enough to lead us to where we want to go.

When it comes to following our inner light, it's important to first turn it on. We do this by naming in what area we want or are open to inner guidance. Once we openly acknowledge that we want guidance and in what specific areas, our intuition can then dial in and start to lead us there. In speaking out and asking for guidance, we move past our own inner mental or emotional resistance more quickly than otherwise and fall into a state of listening to and cooperation with our authentic Spirit.

Many people do fear, deep down, that following their intuition will completely deconstruct, if not destroy, their lives. That rationale isn't entirely off base. If you've built your life on fearful choices that have led you away from your authentic Self, you know it. And you also know deep down in your heart of hearts that the minimum amount of genuine focus inward will make you painfully aware of this. Yet what you don't realize is that your Spirit isn't a "gotcha" machine, ready to pounce on you and point out your mistakes without also offering a help line. Rather, your intuition is the inner light that reorients your path and sprinkles it with creative ideas about ways to get back on course.

Ignoring or resisting your intuition is just your ego's way of not allowing the greater, more deeply empowered authentic you to come alive. The trouble, though, is that if you refuse to acknowledge your intuition, your life patterns and problems won't shift or improve. It is only by acknowledging your inner voice on a daily basis that your life will change.

Start with a few moments of quiet breathing, meditation, and perhaps a few yoga stretches that quiet and center your body. Then reach as deep as you can within you and speak out the truth that flows forth—unedited. At first, the answers may be less than inspired: "My heart says, 'I'm hungry,'" or "My heart says, 'This feels stupid.'" But give it time, and when your resistance is fully breached, you'll be amazed by the unexpected yet profound wisdom that spontaneously emerges. In this way you'll be able to directly experience the power and guidance of Spirit as it shows you how to improve your life without bringing catastrophe upon you. Your intuition doesn't invite misery—it simply points out what is making you miserable now and suggests a different way, one that will bring you back to inner peace and joy if you give it a chance.

Philip and I worked to get him back to living more in alignment with his Spirit. We acknowledged his true desire to go in the direction of landscape design full-time, something his Spirit yearned for, although he was sure it wouldn't support him in the same comfortable and predictable way his consulting job did, if at all. By inviting Philip to breathe past his resistance and fear and tune in to his Spirit for guidance about how to safely proceed in this desired direction, a new door opened for him.

One day, after just a few meditative deep breaths and turning inward to listen to his intuition, he flashed upon a sudden new insight that he later shared with me in an excited phone call. "I had this epiphany today! It came out of nowhere," he gushed enthusiastically, "as to how I could start a business in landscape design by keeping two or three strong clients on a freelance basis until I'm established. I even saw which clients I should reach out to. And better yet, I know without a doubt that I'm invaluable to them, so they'll agree to keep working with me in this new capacity. In fact, I actually enjoy working with them, so I'd be happy to stay on with them! I feel it so strongly that I'm going to go with it." It felt so right, he insisted, that he had to at least explore it.

The minute he acknowledged, out loud, what his Spirit genuinely wanted, his intuition took the next step and showed him the way to make that happen. But until he chose to openly acknowledge his true desire, and tune in to his intuition for guidance to show the way, all he experienced was a vicious cycle of mental confusion, stagnation, and frustration, and what appeared like endless roadblocks to his true goals—all of which did nothing but exhaust him.

## Tuning In

Your mind wants you to believe that acknowledging your intuition is impractical, a waste of time, and possibly dangerous; and it will do everything to keep you distracted. After all, paying attention to your intuition would potentially change everything (and you know that your thinking mind fears change). Your intuition points out what isn't genuinely in alignment with your authentic Self and guides you back to center. As you develop the habit of openly acknowledging your intuition, you'll also be shown the way in which to best put it into action.

It may take a moment or two for your mental chatter to quiet down so you can hear. Be patient, because it will. Relax as you tune in. Your Spirit has powerful guidance to offer, so give it your full attention at least for a few minutes. Be aware of any and all intuitive hits, bright ideas, flashes, or creative thoughts that may cross your mind. They will arise quickly and leave just as quickly, so it's important to notice and acknowledge them, however subtle they may be. You may hear them in your mind; or you might hear, see, or simply feel them. Or all of the above!

Once you've tuned in, verbally acknowledge all these subtle flashes of insight and intuition, in whatever guise they appear. Affirm them out loud as they flash across your mind so that you capture them before they slip away. For example, while driving to work, ask your intuition, out loud, what it says is important to know about the day ahead, and then allow your intuition to answer, again out loud. Yes, I know I'm asking you to talk to yourself, but it's your authentic Self that gets to answer, and that feels wonderful! If you are having difficulties with a client or partner or family member, ask out loud, "How can I best deal with this person? What am I missing or unaware of that I need to know in order to improve our relationship and get past this problem?" Then, place your hand on your heart, where intuition is centered and quickly answer, out loud, allowing your Spirit to speak.

Another way to invite your intuition to speak is to mentally conduct an energetic body scan, and when you run into a feeling of tense, restless, or agitated energy anywhere in your body, ask yourself, out loud, what this energy is trying to tell you. Then answer out loud. If you answer, "I don't know," ask again, only this time saying, "If you were to know, what is this energy trying to tell me?" and answer quickly, before you have time to think. Don't make this exercise too difficult. Just say whatever comes to your mind first. Don't try to get the "right" answer. Simply tune in to and allow whatever comes through without mental control or censoring. Be curious about what your inner voice has to say. It will have a lot to offer if you give it a chance to speak freely.

Once you vocalize your intuitive flashes, you'll soon see they have real value. You don't have to do anything else. Just acknowledge your vibes out loud, letting them sink in. Allow yourself to acknowledge your intuition without having to justify it. Simply notice and express what you feel and see what happens.

When you develop the daily habit of openly expressing your intuition, you'll find it offers up more and more direction. It's like opening up a long-closed tap. At first the water may flow in spurts, but soon it just keeps on coming and gets clearer and clearer by the moment. Many people believe intuition gives you the whole picture from the beginning, but it never works that way. Intuition guides you, step-by-step. It cannot show you the next step until you take the first one. Fortunately, the first is easy to take. Just speak the truth from your heart. By doing so, you admit that your intuition is real and you're tuning in, loud and clear. Just try it for five minutes and see for yourself how once you start to acknowledge your intuition, it miraculously "turns on" and starts to flow, giving you moment-to-moment guidance that addresses every challenge you will face as you return to living your true and authentic Spirit.

### Asking the Questions

Close your eyes and calmly breathe in and out through your nose. Start with a sigh or two to help you relax. Massage your jaw and throat a little to release even more tension and fear held in that part of your body, your expression center. Feel the energetic tension that your racing mind creates in your body. Do you notice how it drains your energy, your life force, your kefi, right out of you?

Now relax the tension in your neck and throat as much as possible with a few gentle stretches and take in a deep, easy, belly-filling breath. Don't force your breath to enter your body by raising your shoulders and holding your head back. Rather, keep your shoulders comfortably relaxed and down, and allow your belly to pull the air in naturally without any tension at all. Exhale by releasing the sound "Ah," and then bring the corners of your lips up to your ears in a gentle smile.

Next, take out your journal and tune inward. Contemplate each of the following questions, and invite your Spirit, your most enlightened Self, to respond to each one. Give yourself plenty of time to sense and feel the genuine response arising from your heart, the true source of your power.

- Do you have a regular habit of openly acknowledging your intuition?

- Do you engage in a specific practice or ritual for tuning in to your Spirit every day?

- In what specific ways do you tune in to your intuition throughout the day?

- Do you begin your day by connecting with your Spirit? Describe your practice.

- Do you tune in to your inner guidance before you make decisions? If yes, describe how you do so. If not, what might help you begin to do this?

- Do you end your day by acknowledging the guidance you received? Do you quietly write it down in a journal or speak it out loud? If not, what might help make this easier for you to do?

- Do you have a daily practice for tuning inward and simply being with your Spirit, through daily meditation, gentle breathing, praying, stretching, walking, or easy yoga, for example? In other ways? If not, what might help make this possible? What are the greatest obstacles to tuning in to your Spirit right now?

- In what areas of your life do you most often doubt that your intuition is safe to trust or follow? Do you feel threatened? In what way exactly? Even though you may feel that trusting your intuition is somewhat

threatening to your sense of security, are you really
threatening or just extremely uncomfortable at the
thought of risking a change?

- Are there areas where you refuse or are afraid to trust
your intuition to guide you? Around money matters,
for example? In your relationships? With certain
family members, such as with your parents or your
teenage children?

After writing down your answers, set aside your journal and
remain seated. Close your eyes, and calmly breathe in and out
through your nose. Start by releasing a sigh or two to help you
relax. Relax the tension in your jaw by gently massaging it for
a moment. Take note of the changing vibration in your body
after contemplating how your life might be different if you were
to begin a daily practice of centering yourself on your powerful
guiding Spirit. Can you feel the relief that comes from looking
inward to your authentic Spirit for support and guidance—and
not relying upon uninformed or unconscious others for direction
in your life?

With your next breath, let all of your tension go and simply *be* for a moment or two, even longer if possible. Enjoy sitting
and breathing deeply, empty of all thought, free of any agenda,
centered in the moment. Feel this vibration of being connected,
through your heart space, to your authentic Spirit. Notice how
peaceful, content, and even energized this feels. This is the power
of your Spirit, and it's available to you at all times. It is the real
you. *Remember and believe this.*


### Daily Ritual: Try Connected Breathing

As simplistic and repetitious as it sounds, *breathing* is the most
effective action to interrupt and actually end the ego's game of
fear and control and help you connect with your authentic Self.
Through gentle conscious breathing you can elevate your personal

vibration to a higher, more creative, empowered, and enlightened level. Gentle focused breathing is the quickest way to tune in to your intuition as well as connect to your expanded, joyful Spirit.

My favorite breathing technique to connect with my intuition is called *connected breathing,* a technique I learned by taking a "Transformational Breath" workshop with a woman named Judith Kravitz several years ago. It is also written about in a book called *The Presence Process* by Michael Brown.

It's very simple, and I do it every morning, and again when I feel troubled and need to clear my mind and tune in to inner guidance on specific matters. Here's the process: Wake up 15 minutes earlier than you normally would. Sit up in bed, with your back against a pillow. If possible, set your alarm to ring after 15 minutes, so you can relax and focus without worrying about running late.

Close your eyes, and take a few deep breaths in and out through your nose to gently wake up your body. Pull your breath even more deeply into your abdomen by relaxing your diaphragm as you inhale. Then quickly release your breath by relaxing your muscles, as if letting out a sigh. (Continue breathing through your nose, keeping your mouth shut.) Don't force your breaths either way, but do be aware of allowing each inhalation to enter deep into your belly, and then releasing it easily and quickly.

As you breathe, connect the end of each inhale with the beginning of each exhale, and vice versa, so that there is no pause between breaths. It may feel odd at first, especially since you're probably used to unconsciously holding your breath. By connecting your breathing, you also connect to the nonstop flow of Divine Spirit, which clears and quiets your mind and activates your intuition. Soon you'll get used to this technique and enjoy the way it makes you feel.

It helps to visualize your breath flowing in and out of your body as a swinging pendulum: inhale, breath swinging in; exhale, breath swinging out. Imagine your breath flowing easily and peacefully in and out of your lungs, over and over again, without interruption, for 15 minutes.

With practice, you'll enter a trancelike state in a few short minutes. See yourself pulling in Divine love with every inhalation, energizing every cell in your body with vitality and holiness. Notice how available to each breath your body is. As you exhale, do so gently and without force. Imagine releasing all the toxins circulating in your system back into the atmosphere, along with any anxiety, stress, worry, toxic thinking, negative past experiences, and free-floating fears of the future that reside inside you. See each exhale energetically purging all choices and behaviors that no longer serve a useful and positive purpose in your life, and each inhale fueling your authentic Self in every way.

Know that your flowing breath is cleansing you, inside and out, creating a cocoon of brilliant life-giving, guiding energy all around you. Feel the shift in vibration that it creates. The deeper and longer you focus on your breathing, the more clear your body, mind, and emotions become, and the sharper your intuition becomes. This leaves you relaxed, peaceful, confident, and fully grounded in the present.

Continue doing this connected breath technique until the alarm rings. Then rub your hands together, place them gently over your closed eyes, and focus on the peacefulness flowing through your body. Don't rush or change your breathing pattern. Gently massage the area around your closed eyes for a moment or two. Slowly open your eyes, and look at your palms. Blink once or twice to refocus on the world around you. Then, with a final deep breath, slowly pull your hands away from your eyes and look around the room. Stretch, slowly stand up, and resume normal breathing.

As you start the day, feel how you're fully supported by the Divine love and joyful Spirit within you. The more you practice making this inner connection, the less troubled you will be by your own fearful thoughts, and the more grounded and less insecure you will feel. Conscious breathing centers you on your true source of guidance and power. Use connected breathing whenever you feel uncomfortable, possessed by negative thoughts, in doubt, unsafe, or unsure of yourself and you'll return to this peaceful, holy state of inward, grounded guidance in a matter of a few short minutes.

## A Gut Feeling

As you begin to dig deep in search of your inner truth and guidance, you may come across much that has no real value to you, even if others tell you it does. Another's treasure will never be your own, and other people's advice, no matter how well intended, can never substitute for the guidance of your own intuition. Sometimes you must dig yourself out from under others' beliefs, values, and influences and find your way back to your truth, your Spirit.

Andrea was raised with her twin sister and two other siblings by highly intellectual and politically active parents who lived and worked under the umbrella of the University of Chicago, a world-renowned academic institution. She loved reading, learning, and engaging in lively debates with a diverse group of teachers and students from around the world who often stayed in her family's home for weeks or even months at a time.

As a child, Andrea was independent, outspoken, and creative. From the age of 6 through her early 20s, she studied dance. It was her passion. She was excited to embark on a life of professional dancing after college, until her mother repeatedly commented that it was time for her to get serious and find a "real job" after graduation. Dejected after this intense campaign against her dream, Andrea simply hung up her dancing shoes and shut the door on something she truly loved. Thus began what she called her "lost years." She drifted from one job to the next in several nonprofit agencies, trying to engage in "meaningful" work. But each one was more devoid of life-giving energy and genuine meaning than the last.

After 20 years of frustration and periods of unemployment, Andrea refused to indulge her dissatisfaction any longer and forged ahead in search of a career she could really connect with.

Drawing upon her activist interests, she finally decided to return to school and pursue a degree in public policy. This ambition satisfied her ego's need to attain something of "social substance" and might finally meet with her mother's long withheld approval. She went back to her roots and applied to the graduate school at the University of Chicago and, to her utter shock, was accepted into the program.

Once the glamour and excitement of this impressive accomplishment wore off, the real work in beginning a new path commenced. To Andrea's horror, what she actually encountered wasn't the meaningful, nurturing work to help shape the world that she had expected; rather, she faced a mountain of sterile, dry intellectual and mathematical studies, which didn't at all speak to her interests, let alone her Spirit.

To exacerbate the situation, she began to experience flare-ups of intense digestive trouble, something she had dealt with in the past but had managed to keep under control. Almost overnight—shortly after her commitment to the public-policy program—her physical health completely broke down. She couldn't eat a single morsel of food without experiencing severe abdominal pain. She had allergic reactions to foods, chemicals, and sometimes even the air itself. In addition, she couldn't sleep and had no energy; she noticed that her hair was falling out, and she had asthma attacks. She was basically incapacitated.

In a matter of weeks after beginning her studies, Andrea became so ill she had to take a leave of absence from the graduate program and fight for her life. At one point, she turned to her twin sister and said, "I'm dying. Every part of me—mind, body, and soul—has collapsed. I can't get myself to rally or turn it around like I've done before. I'm really scared."

For the next two years, Andrea's sole focus was on getting well. She visited ten specialists in the hope of receiving a diagnosis and cure. Instead, she was given ten different opinions, ranging from having multiple sclerosis to suffering from depression to making the entire thing up.

During this time, Andrea held on to her public-policy ambitions, but she repeatedly confided in her sister that it appealed more to her intellect than to her gut feeling about what she should dedicate herself to. Not making the connection between her life direction and her illness, she toiled on looking for answers. Finally, she met a holistic doctor who correctly diagnosed her illness as a case of "leaky gut," put her on a massively restricted diet, gave her a ton of books to read, and suggested she begin acupuncture in place of medication to control her symptoms since the medications weren't working.

That meeting changed her life. With the correct diagnosis, she finally relaxed, intuitively sensing that help was on the way. Still unable to return to school, she stayed home and read everything her doctor gave her about her condition. Then she read books on nutrition, holistic healing, and getting in touch with her *chi,* her Spirit, her ultimate Source of vitality. In the process, an entirely new world slowly unveiled itself to her. The things she was learning, along with a gradual improvement in her health, began to make a big difference in her, both inside and out. She was starting to heal not only her body, but also her restless, anxious, "got to do something meaningful right now," intellectually driven mind as well.

As she became stronger, Andrea began to review her life from a new perspective, one that approached her physical health as a reflection of her spiritual health. She could trace the first symptoms of her poor health all the way back to the very week she walked away from dance, her authentic love, and shut that door to her Spirit. The more she had pursued interests and jobs that only appealed to her intellect (and completely ignored her intuition and authentic Self), the more frequent and worse her symptoms had become.

One day, soon after a particularly healing session with her acupuncturist, Andrea called her twin sister and said she needed to come over. Once there, not even sure what she was thinking, let alone what she was going to say, she suddenly blurted out, "I don't want to return to the University of Chicago and study public policy. I think I want to study acupuncture instead."

Her own words surprised her. She hadn't known she felt that way! After all, it was completely different from anything she'd ever done or expressed interest in before. Yet now, deeply immersed in her healing journey, she realized that these words were the first she uttered that felt right in her gut. In fact, once she announced her feelings out loud, her entire body buzzed with a burst of energy, as if to say, *Yes! That's so true!*

Andrea's twin didn't miss a beat. "Look at you. You're beaming! There's a light in your eyes that I haven't seen for at least two years, maybe more. I think it means that quitting the university path and studying the alternative is exactly what you must do. Follow your intuition!"

And that was that. Andrea's decision was made. But more than that, for the first time in her life, it was a decision made by her Spirit—her authentic Self, and not just her intellect wanting to impress and please her critical mother. The following day, she withdrew from school and signed up for training in acupuncture and Chinese medicine. At 50 years old, she'd never felt more alive, passionate, and enthusiastic about her life as in that moment.

A year later, Andrea's body had completely recovered, and the light in her eyes had grown brighter than ever. She loves her training program, which is demanding and rigorous, but truly aligned with her Spirit. She's even feeling an intuitive urge to start her own practice. When talking to her over dinner recently, I asked her exactly what had happened to cause her to completely change her path.

She paused for a moment and then said, "From the time I was young, my world was centered on the intellect. Feelings weren't highly regarded, and intuition, let alone Spirit, was something we didn't accept or believe in at all. I guess I confused it with religion, and wouldn't ever entertain such superstition as an intellectual person. And yet, it took me nearly dying to open my mind and heart to what I'd denied for so long.

"Don't get me wrong. I still love science, activism, and health care; and I'll always have an intellectual mind-set. I just discovered that there was a missing component: tuning in to and following my heart and inner guidance. When I discovered that, my life began healing from the inside out. From the time I quit dance, I hadn't had any means to express my inner feelings, and because of that, I eventually began to wither and die. But once I opened up to my intuition and began to listen, everything started to improve."

We all eventually reach a moment in life when we must come face-to-face with a force greater than our ego shielding, or intellect; at that point, we're invited to recognize the intuitive guiding force of our Spirit. People struggle against this because they've been taught to. And they resist coming back to it because they've been told it's not "real" and don't want to feel foolish or risk appearing crazy. So they rebel against themselves. And *that* is crazy! On the contrary, listening to our intuition and allowing ourselves to follow what we feel in our deepest Self is the only guarantee of real health and happiness we have. It's the most intelligent, powerful, brilliant, authentic, sane choice we can make.

### Tuning In

As you begin to dig in more deeply to discover and heed your inner voice, be open and responsive to all the wonderful ways in which your intuition is presently speaking to you. For example, notice the messages that fleet across your path, such as on the side of a bus or on the license plate of the car in front of you, suggesting things like, "Call your mom," or "Time to step up." Follow, rather than resist, the impulse to reach for a book or sign up for classes on any subject that you intuitively feel drawn to—such as energy healing, landscape gardening, or playing a musical instrument, for instance—and would love to bring into your life.

The more you begin to notice the subtle yet ever-present signals from your inner Self reaching out to you through various and often even amusing ways, the more you will be amazed by the regularity and humor with which they show up.

Do something different and say yes to the daylong workshop happening in your area on the subject your heart longs to learn more about and incorporate into your life. Listen to live webcasts hosted by spiritual teachers and thinkers that are brought to your attention. Take it a step further and commit to learning more about your intuition and how to better tune in to your vibes by joining an in-depth class that allows you to practice recognizing and expressing more fully your intuition with others in a safe container. It's no accident that once you decide to open up to your intuition, doors seem to miraculously open all around to support your decision.

You may think it's a coincidence that certain events or new opportunities are suddenly opening up to you, but the truth is that they were there all along. It was you who hadn't yet been open or tuned in to this before now. Yet, as it's been said, once the student is ready, the teacher (in all its forms) appears. You're stepping through the doorway to Spirit, back to your enlightened Self, and are now preparing to take the leap and follow your inner guidance.

Openly and vocally acknowledge all intuitive impulses and respond to every vibe you feel, even the ones that seem "crazy." Don't worry about whether or not your intuition is "right." Instead ask yourself, *What feels true for me right now?* And go with that. Tune inward and wait for guidance to come from your heart. Quiet your mind enough to hear the answers, and be brave enough to consider them.

### Asking the Questions

Close your eyes and calmly breathe in and out through your nose. Start with a sigh or two to help you relax. Massage your jaw and throat a little to release even more tension and fear held in that part of your body, your expression center. Feel the energetic tension that your racing mind creates in your body. Do you notice how it drains your energy, your life force, your kefi, right out of you?

Now relax the tension in your neck and throat as much as possible with a few gentle stretches and take in a deep, easy, belly-filling breath. Don't force your breath to enter your body by raising your shoulders and holding your head back. Rather, keep your shoulders comfortably relaxed and down, and allow your belly to pull the air in naturally without any tension at all. Exhale by releasing the sound "Ah," and then bring the corners of your lips up to your ears in a gentle smile.

Next, take out your journal and tune inward. Contemplate each of the following questions, and invite your intuition, your Spirit, to respond to each one. Give yourself plenty of time to feel the genuine response coming from your heart, the source of your power.

- In what ways has your intuition guided you today?

- What might your Spirit be conveying to you, through subtle impulses or "inklings," that you are ignoring or aren't giving your full attention to?

- Do you feel a conflict between your Spirit (your most authentic Self) and your intellect (your rational mind)? If so, can you describe this discord?

- Were you given strong ideas about the way you "should " or are "supposed to" act or behave by your parents, teachers, or other authority figures in the past? Were these beliefs subtly implied or overtly enforced? How do you feel about these beliefs today?

- Do you feel any internal conflict between what you feel you "should do" according to your mind or others' opinions, and what you feel called in your heart to do? How strong is the conflict?

- How strongly do you presently feel the intuitive urge to expand, create, or express yourself in a new or different way? Do you spend lots of time mentally trying to figure things out to no peaceful avail?

- Do you take time to tune inward and quietly listen to your Spirit? Do you tune in to your intuition and listen for guidance on specific things? In certain areas over others? For others over yourself or vice versa?

- Are you afraid of or do you feel slightly threatened by what your intuition might reveal or suggest to improve your life?

After writing down your answers, set aside your journal and remain seated. Close your eyes and calmly breathe in and out through your nose. Start with a sigh or two to help you relax. Reflect on the vibration in your body after contemplating the conflict between ego and Spirit.

With your next breath, let go of all of your tension and simply *be* for a moment or two, even longer if possible. Enjoy sitting and breathing deeply, empty of all thought, free of any agenda, centered in the moment. Feel this vibration of being connected to Source. Notice how peaceful, content, and even energized you feel. This is the power of your Spirit, and it's available to you at all times. It is the real you. *Remember and trust this.*

### Daily Ritual: Peel the Onion

Tuning in to your deepest knowing is much like peeling away the layers of an onion. Each layer represents what is not your authentic and true Self. Practice connected breathing and visualize what might make up your layers. Your outer layer might be anger or anxiety, for example. Peel it away with your breath. Maybe the next layer is control or frustration. Again, breathe deeply and peel that away, as well. The next layer might be confusion or fear. Continue peeling away each layer of negative energy that's occupying your mind—one at a time—until you reach your heart, your Spirit.

The layers may peel off quickly, or they might barely budge. Don't worry about it—just notice where the layers stick and whether it's a thought, feeling, belief, or old pattern controlling you at the moment. When you hit a block, sit with it, breathe into it, and observe it nonjudgmentally. Pay attention to the energy and how it controls you. Notice how your thought pattern feels, too. Your ego keeps you stuck in patterns that cause energetic contractions, inhibiting your breathing and interrupting the flow of life. Watch these patterns as you continue gently breathing.

If you're experiencing particularly intense emotions—such as anger, fear, insecurity, sadness, or anxiety—simply keep breathing and see how connected breathing and awareness affect them. Be still and observe. Do not act on any energy that might feel as though it is engulfing you; remember to just breathe and observe. Notice how, with each inhale and exhale, you're able to put more space and light between yourself and any intense thoughts and feelings you may have at the moment.

Continue unpeeling the layers as you breathe for at least three to five minutes (ten if possible). This is usually enough time to break free of the trance that ego patterns put you in. The quiet observer in you is your Spirit. With each breath of awareness, you'll realize how much stronger, brighter, and more powerful your inner voice becomes. Each breath ushers in more space and light, releasing you from the grip of fear and anxiety.

By tuning in to your intuition every day for a few minutes, you'll automatically start responding differently to the challenges before you. What might have felt intimidating before tuning in to your intuition may start to feel more manageable, as you spontaneously tune more quickly in to solutions over worry about these matters. Be patient with your progress in the beginning. Shifting from a mental reaction to a deeper Spirit-guided response takes a bit of time. Your experience won't change overnight, but with consistent practice you'll see a *big* difference in a matter of days.

The biggest shift will come if you can make a sustained commitment to peeling away the layers of doubt and fear and tuning in to your intuition for the next 40 days. That may seem like more than you can promise, but don't judge in advance. Give it a try, one day at a time, and if you have a positive result that day, tune in again the next day, working toward 40 consecutive days. The reason I suggest a 40-day duration is that this length of time is mentioned many times throughout the Bible and represents a full season or cycle of change. If you practice peeling away the layers of your fearful self and tuning in to your inner guiding Spirit for a full 40 days, you will succeed in overriding your old patterns and establishing a new Spirit-centered way of life.

When you begin to flow in harmony with your inner guidance, you experience a remarkable liberation from being controlled by unwanted ego patterns. The more you apply observant breathing techniques, the more quickly you will break free from unproductive negative thoughts and enter the clear, expanded, creative guiding light of your Spirit.

### Better Than Disneyland

As you return to an authentic life, you may face disapproval from those who don't support your newly awakened state. It's important to trust your intuition anyway as it guides you in digging out of a life that is familiar, but no longer feels authentic for you. Find your courage and know that your commitment to dig your way out of soul-stifling conditions will pay off in recovering your true Self and inner joy.

Lexy's life was simple and she never questioned the way things were. Born and raised in a small rural town in Tennessee—in the heart of the Bible Belt—she followed the strict rules of her Baptist upbringing. She worked in an office after graduating from high school and never went to college. At 19, she married John, a nice guy she'd met in church, and had three beautiful sons with him, one right after the other.

Her life as a stay-at-home mom was her world, and as far as she knew, this was what life was all about. So Lexy was happy . . . until one day, just moments after her husband called to say he was on his way home from work, a large tractor unexpectedly pulled out in front of his car, causing a terrible accident. John died instantly, and so did everything that Lexy knew or believed about life.

She felt stunned, confused, abandoned, and devastated. This wasn't what her life was supposed to be like. According to the "life script" she was taught and followed obediently, they were supposed to raise their kids together and take vacations at the lake each summer. John was going to coach Little League, and she would host the kids' birthday parties. They would add on to the house and grow old together. But now all that had disappeared. Without her husband, Lexy felt as if she could hardly function. Her world had been torn apart, and life would never be the same again.

Fortunately, her husband was well insured, so at least Lexy was able to meet the family's financial needs without further destabilizing all of their lives. She just had to pick up the shattered pieces of herself and put them back together again—and fast, because her kids needed her. But she didn't know where or how to start doing that.

The town where she lived offered little support or comfort. It seemed in many ways that her neighbors were far more interested in gossiping about the accident—whispers of "the poor thing" seemed to follow her everywhere—than they were in actually helping her regain her footing once the funeral was over. It's not that they weren't nice people. They just didn't know how to comfort her after such a shocking tragedy, so they avoided her instead.

Lexy found even less support at her church. Every time she went, it seemed as if all she heard about was sin and damnation, but next to nothing about heaven. Where was her husband now that his life was over? Was he in hell, as her preacher suggested? How could that be? Her anxious thoughts consumed her and became so disturbing that they even gave her nightmares. She stopped going to church, even though that gave the town's residents something else to gossip about.

Never once before this accident did she even think to question what she'd heard from the pulpit every Sunday throughout her entire life. But after John died, she couldn't listen to a word of it. Something inside her told her that it just wasn't true.

So Lexy was left on her own to figure out what was true so that she could escape this nightmare, but she didn't know where to start. She began her search for understanding and a way to connect with others in the most accessible place she knew: *The Oprah Winfrey Show*. One day, the show featured a few guests who had appeared in the movie *The Secret*. Lexy listened to them discussing "the Spirit within," which was a radically new concept to her. The only Spirit she knew of was the Holy Spirit, whom she greatly feared and would certainly never be so audacious as to consider a part of herself, as these people were suggesting. She wasn't worthy—no one was. It was almost heretical.

Intrigued, and fueled by her pain and a need for answers, she overcame her hesitation and ordered the movie as well as some of the books that were also discussed on the show. On that day, the door to the nonphysical world cracked open for Lexy. The heaven and hell she was taught to believe in slowly began to disappear, and she took the first steps toward courageously pushing past her fears and hesitations in search of her husband's Spirit so she could at least say good-bye and find some closure.

The discovery process commenced. One spiritual book led to another and another, until Lexy had read all that the local bookstore had to offer (which wasn't much). She moved her search on to the Internet, looking for more material from which she could find answers. Not only did she become a voracious reader of all topics spiritual—including life after death, reincarnation, thoughts and beliefs and how they shape our lives, positive manifestation, and more—but she also began to subscribe and listen to countless online radio shows featuring all kinds of exciting and enlightening interviews relating to spirituality.

The more she learned, the more she wanted to know. Each tidbit she picked up about the world beyond the physical and the notion of a Spirit within eased the gaping wound in her heart a little more. Although she was finally beginning to feel better, she soon discovered that her newfound views couldn't be happily shared with others. In fact, people in her town thought she'd lost her mind and her religion, and that she was either crazy, possessed by the devil due to the emotional trauma from the accident, or just plain weird. Her neighbors smiled politely when face-to-face with her, but many gossiped even more the minute she was out of earshot.

Lexy's pain, however, was too great for her to worry about what others thought or try to regain their approval. She was sinking, and her kids needed her to stay afloat. Following her intuition and learning all she could about spirituality was the only thing that helped, and it helped her a lot.

Although her mind had calmed somewhat knowing that everyone has an eternal, holy Spirit that doesn't die, she didn't feel the Spirit *in her*. But she desperately wanted to. In fact, she needed to, so she decided to search for ways to succeed in her quest no matter what it took. She had to feel the guidance of her Spirit so she could teach her kids to feel it, too. Then they'd never be as afraid of, and as unprepared for, sudden change and death, as she had been. She never wanted them to go through the hell she was slowly starting to come out of. She realized that she could never prevent her children from facing sorrow and loss in life, but she could at least equip them with the spiritual wherewithal to know how to deal with it so that it wouldn't destroy them as it almost did her.

Lexy pushed herself even further into the unknown and stepped out of her comfort zone by enrolling in several online spiritual classes so that she could connect with others with similar interests. She chatted with people from all over the world, many of whom were enduring dramatic life changes, as she was, which confirmed that she wasn't alone or crazy—something she had wondered about from time to time.

Soon, however, even web classes weren't enough to satisfy Lexy's relentless curiosity and insatiable desire to know her Spirit. She started feeling claustrophobic in her small town and wanted to be with others she could share and compare ideas with in person. So doing the unthinkable for mothers in her community, she left her kids with her mother and went to a weeklong seminar on spirituality and intuition in upstate New York, all the while mindful of the gossip and scorn that trailed in her wake.

Miraculously, she didn't care. Her heart was healing and her world was expanding. And even more exciting and unexpected, she actually felt closer to her husband in Spirit than she ever had before. They'd never had an intimate conversation while he was alive, let alone shared anything about their Spirit. It simply didn't come up because they weren't aware of it. Now, every night, she could connect with his Spirit in her heart and feel his presence, however subtle and fleeting. She no longer doubted. He was helping her from the spirit realm to awaken her own Spirit before she died.

*Maybe that's why he died so suddenly,* she thought one day. *He really is helping me, and with all that I'm learning, perhaps I can open the boys up to a richer, more wonderful world than he ever had.*

Propelled by a force seemingly greater than herself, she went from classes and seminars to working personally with gifted massage therapists, energy workers, clairvoyants, intuitives (where she met me), and even shamans. Each healer helped her get a bit closer to her inner voice, her Spirit, and each experience she had helped to reshape and define her new and less limited reality a little more. The cold, rigid, small world she had formerly lived in gave way to what she described as "a trip better than the one my family took to Disneyland when John was alive."

When I asked her to explain in greater depth what she was discovering, she said, "I'm realizing that it's absolutely true that we're guided spiritual beings. I haven't fully gotten my head wrapped around that fact quite yet, but when I'm not in my head, I know it's true. I feel my inner guidance—my Spirit—and it feels as if I'm the brightest, most beautiful light on the planet. I love me. I love others. I love life, and I'm no longer afraid. It's crazy to try to explain my experience because there aren't many words that can really describe what I'm discovering. Words somehow seem inadequate.

"The wild thing is I've never felt more alive, yet I would have never reached this expanded realm had John not died. We were both missing it completely. I realize now that his passing was—after my grief lifted—the greatest gift he ever gave both me and the kids. And now we thank him every day. I finally understand the line from the Bible: 'He died so that we may live.' It's true in our lives. Today we are really living, and before that we were merely existing."

### Tuning In

As you begin to dig deeper for meaning and connection with your guiding Spirit, everything that holds you back or no longer serves a purpose in your soul's growth starts to die off. This pruning process may show up as a loss of interest in certain activities that once held your attention, or it might reveal itself in your experiencing increasing impatience with certain people with whom you no longer seem to energetically resonate. It may show up in an intense need to be free of your given profession or the role you play for others, such as no longer being interested in being a caretaker, or staying in marriage or relationship.

Sometimes what is ready to die shows up unexpectedly and without warning such as it was with Lexy. Sometimes it is you who needs an experience or connection to die off and so you bring about the end yourself. Just as there are times when a dead branch falls off of a tree naturally or as a result of an intense storm, there are other times when we see the need to intervene and cut down a branch that is dying ourselves. So, too, is it with conditions in our lives. No matter how the dying-off process occurs in your life, when it does, you will feel your Spirit's authentic pulse seeking to beat in your heart once again. At these junctions, and in spite of the stress such dying processes can bring about, you nevertheless do eventually sense in your heart a definite reach toward something greater, something more empowering being born in you.

This "dying off" experience I'm referring to, however, is not to be confused with the act of withdrawing or shutting yourself away from life due to depression, which is a closing off from life as opposed to opening up to something greater. If you find yourself consciously withdrawing from life due to depression, please have compassion for yourself and ask your Spirit to help you reach out for the support you need to help you move through this difficult passage. Depression can be treated, and your Spirit can help in every facet of that healing process if you allow it.

As we reclaim our true inner power, it is natural that those aspects of our lives that we've outgrown or no longer reflect our evolution do die off. We all undergo emotional, intellectual, and ultimately, physical death as we are born to the unlimited experience of embracing our Divine nature. These mini-deaths are frightening and tragic to the ego but liberating to the Spirit. Just as a caterpillar must first release its old form before it can transform into the emancipated butterfly, life as we know it must also "die" in one form before it reappears in its newly expressed, Divine state.

### Asking the Questions

Close your eyes and calmly breathe in and out through your nose. Start with a sigh or two to help you relax. Massage your jaw and throat a little to release even more tension and fear held in that part of your body, your expression center. Feel the energetic tension that your racing mind creates in your body. Do you notice how it drains your energy, your life force, your kefi, right out of you?

Now relax the tension in your neck and throat as much as possible with a few gentle stretches and take in a deep, easy, belly-filling breath. Don't force your breath to enter your body by raising your shoulders and holding your head back. Rather, keep your shoulders comfortably relaxed and down, and allow your belly to pull the air in naturally without any tension at all. Exhale by releasing the sound "Ah," and then bring the corners of your lips up to your ears in a gentle smile.

Next, take out your journal and tune inward. Contemplate each of the following questions and invite your guiding Spirit, your most authentic and enlightened Self, to respond to each one. Give yourself plenty of time to feel the genuine response coming from your heart, the source of your power.

- What in your life feels as if it is no longer serving you and is, in fact, dying? Are there activities you once loved but are no longer interested in today? Are there people you used to be close with whom you now find intrusive, annoying, superficial, or dull?

- Do you want certain parts of your life to die? Would you be secretly relieved if certain parts of your life did die off? Are you allowing or trusting this end to come? Would you feel secretly relieved?

- Where do you feel most limited? What are you outgrowing?

- Is something new coming in? What is trying to get your attention and teach you something? Are you receptive, or are you refusing to open up to it?

- Who or what has died—literally or symbolically— leaving you to reevaluate your ideas and beliefs about life?

- In what ways has that death or ending opened you up to a new beginning?

- Do you hear your inner voice, or does it feel as if your intuition is silent?

- How might you better support your authentic Spirit and give it new life? (Really take your time on this question and allow your Spirit to answer. It will guide you if you let it.)

After writing down your answers, set aside your journal and remain seated. Close your eyes and calmly breathe in and out through your nose. Start with a sigh or two to help you relax. Think of a time when you let go of an old belief and opened yourself up to a new understanding.

With your next breath, let all of your tension go and simply *be* for a moment or two, even longer if possible. Enjoy sitting and breathing deeply, empty of all thought, free of any agenda, centered in the moment. Feel this vibration of being connected to Source. Notice how peaceful, content, and even energized you feel. This is the power of your guiding Spirit, and it's available to you at all times. It is the real you. *Remember and trust this.*

### Daily Ritual: Let Go

When tuning in to our inner guidance, it becomes evident that we may have to release ourselves from particular ideas, beliefs, attitudes, and even situations. Following the numerous examples in nature—such as snake shedding its skin—look for any attachment that restricts you or causes you unnecessary pain, and ask your Spirit to help you release it in order to allow new energy and solutions to come in. What in your life is no longer serving you and asking to be released today? Can you let it go?

An outworn attachment can be to a person, an attitude, or a limiting belief about someone or something (including yourself). It could be an attachment through fear to an unhappy work situation, an unhappy relationship, a negative judgment about yourself or someone else, or even the need to always get your own way.

If you aren't sure what might be best to release at this moment, don't worry; you'll know soon enough. Simply be *open* to the idea of letting go of any belief, perspective, or behavior that doesn't positively contribute to your life. The more challenging this is, the greater the reward if you do so. To hold on to a position, belief, opinion, conflict, person, or situation when it no longer serves you blocks your intuition and keeps you from flowing in grace in your life. Remember, all that dies returns in a higher form.

One of my favorite rituals for letting go of those things I no longer want in my life is to write them down on pieces of paper and then burn them. As I write about each thing I choose to release, I include everything I feel this thing, person, habit, or experience brought to me in terms of the lessons I learned and the gifts received. Doing this gives me a sense of honorary closure as I move on. After I finish writing everything down, I end by speaking these words: "I now completely and freely release myself from all further connection to this (fill in the blank) and open myself to something better." Then I sign and date it before setting it alight.

I encourage you to try this ritual for anything you want to release as well. If you have a fireplace, use that to burn the paper in. If you don't have a fireplace, be sure to use a safe container and watch it until it completely burns out. If you have more than one thing you seek to let go of, write each on a separate piece of paper, including with it the lessons learned and gifts received. Once you've burned your piece (or pieces) of paper, sit quietly and take a few deep breaths. Then imagine how in releasing the old you are making way for the new. I've done this ritual many times during the course of my life; and each time I do, I feel relieved, refreshed, and filled with a renewed sense of freedom and hope. I believe you will feel the same way.

### The Virtual Healing Tour

More than digging deep, we also have to dive in and commit ourselves to what we discover and put that newly found treasure into practice in our lives. Otherwise, we remain knowledgeable about, but still out of touch with, our intuition and inner treasure.

Eileen was never a confident person. She tried to build up her self-esteem but not very hard. She did her work each day, but never with two feet fully in. She showed up and took care of her responsibilities, but just did enough to get by. A classic under-achiever, she never felt the need to push herself at all.

It was always that way with her, and she didn't consider it a problem. She was an average student in school, making it through college with the minimum passing grades, and immediately went into the hospitality business after graduating. She started as a waitress in the dining room of a beautiful hotel, and eventually worked her way up to the banquet department and assisted at special events. Her path was gradual and steady, advancing one slow step at a time, and while she did her job well enough to keep it, she never felt that it was her passion. She just did as she was told and kept moving along.

One thing she did enjoy in the hospitality industry, however, was the never-ending parade of interesting people, some of whose backgrounds and philosophies about life differed greatly from her own. One of those guests at a special event was Louise Hay, considered by many to be the leader of the New Thought movement. Louise was staying at the hotel while in town to give a talk, and Eileen escorted her to her seat in the banquet on the afternoon of Louise's all-day event. Their brief, friendly conversation led Eileen to attend Louise's lecture that evening, where she was introduced to the world of intuition, spirituality, and metaphysics for the first time. From the moment she took home a signed copy of Louise's book *You Can Heal Your Life,* Eileen was hooked.

She couldn't get enough and began to consume metaphysical and spiritual books like, as she described it, "a kid hooked on sugar." She spent hours in the spiritual section of bookstores on her days off and bought every newly released title that came out on the subject. It wasn't unusual for her to buy three or four books at a time, not to mention those she ordered online or from the many spiritually minded book clubs she'd joined along the way.

Eileen, voracious reader that she now was, eventually became an armchair expert on meditation, knowing every type there was, including mindful meditation, walking meditation, yoga meditation, eating meditation, and everything in between. She learned the importance of being in the moment, the meaning of "Be here now," and the waste of living in the past or future. She was introduced to the third dimension, the fourth dimension, and the fifth! She read all about angels, spirit guides, light beings, ascended masters, and even aliens. Ultimately, she came to believe that what she was reading about was vastly more interesting than the world she lived in.

Eileen's digging eventually led her into the realm of manifestation, where she was introduced to the power of intention as a way to realize one's dreams—messages she found in my book *Your Heart's Desire.* This book attracted her because of the title. She'd read so much over the years that everything had become overwhelmingly complicated. She didn't know what to believe or whom to follow, and she wanted to be sure that she didn't make a mistake. The notion that she could create her dream was very appealing.

Over the years, Eileen accumulated so many spiritual books that she could have opened her own bookstore. She went to work every day as expected, but she didn't feel secure in her job and constantly worried that her boss would fire her at any moment. Her books helped her cope with such disturbing thoughts, so she raced home to them night after night. It was how she released her anxiety.

Eileen must have learned something about manifesting because she actually did get fired after 20 years on the job. She couldn't say it caught her by surprise, because she'd had several run-ins with the newly hired manager of the hotel over the past few months. He wasn't satisfied with her halfhearted performance and repeatedly warned her to improve. So when the day arrived that she received a pink slip, she realized she'd been expecting it. Secretly, she knew that her manager had a valid point. She hadn't gone the distance, and he was the first person in her life to call her on it. Nevertheless, she was so hurt, lost, and ashamed that she withdrew from the world and buried herself even deeper in her reading. She let her husband take care of her and refused to find a new job.

In spite of the countless books Eileen had read over the past two decades, she felt completely lost. She couldn't find her intuitive voice anywhere and hadn't a clue as to where to look next. That's when it became painfully obvious to her that an intellectual pursuit and knowledge of the Spirit wasn't enough to empower a person. Sure, she could recite myriad teachings as if she were an expert, but she hadn't followed through with a single practice (and if she had, she'd done it with the same halfhearted effort as everything else she attempted in life).

It was as if she'd read a million manuals on how to ride a bike but never actually sat on one and started pedaling. Her spiritual journey was a virtual one—the ideas appealing, yet untested and unpracticed in her life. There were no tangible results. Eileen's discovery process had deteriorated into spiritual window-shopping—gazing upon but not actually attaining any of the positive benefits. In the end, she realized that she was no better off than those who were clueless about their Spirit. Perhaps she was even worse off, because although she knew of the power that was there for her, she couldn't get to it.

Eileen's plight is very common. I know a lot of "spiritual junkies" who could put me to shame with their knowledge about the spiritual realm. There are those who could pass as scholars, yet have never applied even one simple spiritual practice they've learned on a regular basis. They remain stuck in their heads, closed off to their hearts, and painfully tuned out to the true joy and power of their intuition. They are lost in the land of "virtual self-discovery" and cannot seem to find their way out. This is because, as Eileen was so acutely reminded, learning involves far more than gathering information or memorizing facts. To really learn something, one must apply the information regularly enough to experience it directly. Eileen admitted that every time she decided to start a new practice, she would do it for a few days, but soon enough, she'd get frustrated and give up—going back to doing what she had always done without taking any responsibility for her transformation.

"My spiritual books were a way to hide from life," she coura-geously admitted after our last conversation. "I could talk the talk so well that no one really asked me to walk the walk. So I didn't! Truthfully, I didn't want to. It took too much effort to change. I didn't want to be that responsible for my life. I wanted to just show up and have others take care of me. And honestly, my way worked up to a point. I showed up for work, and my employer took care of me. I showed up to my marriage, and my husband took care of me. What I haven't 'shown up' for, however, is *myself,* and now nothing is taking care of me. Not even my spiritual books."

I suggested that Eileen take her process of digging deep to a whole new level and give all of her books away, except for ten, at the most. As she herself admitted, her books were a way for her to escape and tune out the world, rather than tune in to her Spirit. At first she balked, almost like a junkie being asked to give up her stash, but eventually she relented, saying, "I know you're right. These books are keeping me from actually listening to my intu-ition and making any real change in my life. I've been making the mistake of thinking that just because I've read something, I know it and it becomes true in my life, but that's not the case. It's time to put to practice what I've learned."

As a messenger of spiritual teachings, I know that books have their place. That's why I write them. They get the message across, but they don't offer an alternative to real learning. They're the manuals to *assist* in one's learning. The real lessons come from firsthand experience. I suggested that rather than read any more books, Eileen should offer an introductory course on spiritual meditation and intuition to her friends.

"We teach best what we're here to learn," I shared with her. "It might feel scary putting together even a simple two-hour course on meditation, or offering a basic course on intuition, but it will make you commit enough to it yourself to convince others to try it."

"But how could I ever do that if I've never really meditat-ed and don't listen to my intuition?" she gasped, horrified by my suggestion.

"There's only one way," I answered. "Prepare for the course by actually meditating and by tuning in and listening to your intuition. Then you can share your authentic experience—all of it. That's learning, and others will benefit from what you share."

At first Eileen laughed nervously, but I knew she was intrigued. She certainly knew enough people who might want to attend such a course. She talked so often about what she'd read that it wouldn't seem odd for her to do such a thing.

I don't know if Eileen followed through or not. I do know, however, that she was ready to have a real discovery process—not just a virtual one. The Universe was asking more of her, and if she didn't genuinely shift, she knew she would be left behind.

"Who knows?" she said, both laughing and sounding relieved as we prepared to hang up the phone. "Maybe my Spirit got me fired so I'd stop faking in front of myself and everyone else. At least now I have to get real, because there's no one to rescue me. My husband is fed up with me, I lost my job because my boss was fed up with me, and now *I'm* fed up with me. I'm ready for *real* change, and I know it begins with me."

"So dig deeper and go for it," I told her. "At least now you've got nothing to lose."

### Tuning In

Digging deep to get more comfortable with your intuition is tremendously exciting and liberating. And yet, to simply talk about getting in touch with your intuition isn't the same thing as actually tuning in and using it. Friends can tell you all about their wonderful trip to Europe, for example, complete with a video documentary and souvenirs, but you won't really discover Europe until you actually go there yourself.

The same holds true for your intuition. You won't really know the power of your inner voice—your guiding Spirit—until you listen to it directly. To genuinely discover the power of your inner voice, stop talking, stop reading, and start tuning in to your heart.

Be silent long enough to hear the guidance of your Spirit within. Then listen. There is no better way to become truly empowered.

### Asking the Questions

Close your eyes and calmly breathe in and out through your nose. Start with a sigh or two to help you relax. Massage your jaw and throat a little to release even more tension and fear held in that part of your body, your expression center. Feel the energetic tension that your racing mind creates in your body. Do you notice how it drains your energy, your life force, your kefi, right out of you?

Now relax the tension in your neck and throat as much as possible with a few gentle stretches and take in a deep, easy, belly-filling breath. Don't force your breath to enter your body by raising your shoulders and holding your head back. Rather, keep your shoulders comfortably relaxed and down, and allow your belly to pull the air in naturally without any tension at all. Exhale by releasing the sound "Ah," and then bring the corners of your lips up to your ears in a gentle smile.

Next, take out your journal and turn your attention inward. Contemplate each of the following questions and invite your Spirit, your most authentic and enlightened Self, to respond to each one. Give yourself plenty of time to tune in to the genuine response coming from your heart, the source of your power.

- What are you called to explore but haven't yet? Why not? What is holding you back? Is there something you feel in your heart but haven't yet admitted?

- Is there any area or subject in which you consider yourself to be an expert and feel that there's little more to learn?

- Are you in the habit of tuning in to your heart? When and how do you do this?

- When seeking guidance, do you first ask others for their opinion, or do you go inward and consult your intuition—your Spirit?

- Does someone else's opinion override your intuition? Whose? Why is this so?

- Have you spent much time reading spiritual books before this one? If so, have you incorporated any of the suggestions or recommendations you learned into your life? How much effort did you put forth?

- How committed are you to tuning in to your intuition? Would you say you are just curious or perhaps very committed?

- Are you willing to tune in to and listen to your intuition for 40 days? Do you plan to just try and see what happens, or are you willing to give it your full effort?

- Are you hiding from your authentic and enlightened Self? In what ways?

After writing down your answers, set aside your journal and remain seated. Close your eyes, and calmly breathe in and out through your nose. Start with a sigh or two to help you relax. Tell yourself that you will no longer put aside tuning in to your intuition.

With your next breath, let all of your tension go and simply *be* for a moment or two, even longer if possible. Enjoy sitting and breathing deeply, empty of all thought, free of any agenda, centered in the moment. Feel this vibration of being connected to your inner strength and power. Notice how peaceful, content, and even energized you feel. There is real power behind your intuition, and it's available to you at all times. It is the voice of the real you. *Remember this.*

### *Daily Ritual: Be Silent*

Take a few moments every day to sit in silence and tune in to your intuition. It can be a moment in the shower or just after parking your car. It can be as you wash your hands before dinner or while you wait for the train on your way home from work. It can be while folding laundry or watering your plants. These moments of tuning in can occur anytime and anyplace. The more you learn to tune in wherever you are, the easier it will become.

There's no need to focus on any particular thing as you do so. Simply listen to your inner voice, much like you would listen to a respected person speaking to you on the phone. Just give your inner voice your full attention. Silently ask what it wants to share with you.

Intuition can be best heard when your mind is silent. If you tune in closely enough, you can actually distinguish the vibration of intuition and Spirit from that of your ego-based thoughts. The vibration of genuine intuition leaves you feeling expanded, calm, grounded, surprised, and inspired; you're left with a peaceful and uplifted heart and a quiet mind. The vibration of the ego, on the other hand, leaves you feeling tense, agitated, restless, and contracted; you're often left with a troubled heart and mind, and a sense of heaviness and fear.

The more you practice sitting in silence for a few short moments each day, tuned inward and listening, the more quickly you can identify these differences in energy and vibration. When silent, you begin to sense the inner calming vibration of Spirit in your entire body. It's warm yet powerful, strong yet relaxed. It is direct, always unconditionally loving. The more you tune in, the more you will recognize it, and the more guided you will become.

❋

Digging deep to discover the power of your intuition is like suddenly entering a magical land where new things are possible and open to you. Just like when you were a student, you've picked up all of your "school supplies" and are ready for the first day of class. But even though you're well prepared for change, remember that until you put your inner guidance into action, until you incorporate your intuition into your life, real change has yet to take place. But once you start tuning in to your vibes, you'll quickly move to the next step in becoming an empowered and divinely guided being: surrendering your ego and personal will over to your inner voice and guidance.

This can be especially challenging, as you need to take the initiative and make the commitment to act on your intuition, which can feel quite scary. Even though you're awake and aware, you must still make the actual choice to trust your Spirit over your fears and let your inner guidance lead your life. After all, although you may have struggled with life up until now and want a change, you're still entering the unknown when following your inner guidance, and there are no guarantees. The challenge of surrendering your ego control over to your inner voice fortunately passes rather quickly. Like jumping off a diving board, the fear and hesitation you feel beforehand is quickly forgotten and replaced by elation once you make the leap to follow your intuition. This sense of elation comes from totally surrendering to your guiding inner light. You'll feel excited and joyful—immediately sensing the return of your inner power—once you begin to release control to your higher Divine Spirit and let it take over.

Before we dive into the next step, I first want to share a beautiful, creative (and very effective) way to help you anchor your awareness to your guiding Spirit every day so that following your intuition becomes easy and effortless.

※　※　※

*Chapter Four*

# CREATING YOUR PERSONAL ALTAR

To genuinely tune in to your Spirit and feel its guiding force, it's important to make it a central part of your life—something you want to turn to automatically without pause or hesitation. One way to help you achieve this is by creating a personal altar in your home and sitting quietly in front of it every day for a few minutes (preferably during peaceful moments in the morning).

There is no right or wrong way to set up an altar—just follow your intuition. What you create should reflect your deepest, most genuine Self. An altar is meant to be a visual reminder for you to go within through prayer, meditation, contemplation, song, or intuitive listening. Set up your altar as a place where you can anchor your attention inward, detach from the outer world for a moment, and instead tune in to the subtle forces of love and guidance arising in your heart. Your altar serves as a place that helps center your awareness on your inner voice and the guiding flow of love and support flowing from Divine Source to your Higher Self and on to you.

An altar is far more than a beautiful "thing" to look at. It is an active doorway to your beautiful guiding Spirit in many profound ways. Sitting at your altar trains your conscious and subconscious mind to let go of familiar mental patterns (which have habitually controlled you) and tune you in to the subtler, more loving, authentic frequency of Spirit. When you sit in prayer or meditation in front of your altar, you're teaching your mind to relax and surrender to the higher power of the Spirit within.

Altars also serve as energetic portals, or openings, to the realm of Spirit. When you enter the sacred energy surrounding an active altar, the veil between the worlds thins and the heavens open up. If you consistently hold the intention of connecting with your Spirit as you sit at your altar, you'll be "spirited away" into a beautiful higher realm. At first, the shift may be so subtle that you hardly notice the changes through your senses, but with repeated visits, your perception of this heightened vibrational frequency will become stronger. And no matter what you may be thinking about when approaching your altar, your mind will quickly become calm, quiet, and clear as you settle before it; and your heart will open as your vibration shifts to one of pure loving-kindness.

With daily practice, you'll actually *feel* yourself entering this sacred opening to the spirit realm the moment you approach your altar; it feels very similar to what you might experience when you approach an altar in a church, temple, or other holy place. If you haven't felt this or don't think you're energetically sensitive enough to feel it, be patient. Sitting for a few minutes each day in the energy of your personal altar will heighten your awareness, and you'll start to feel this higher vibration. Also, the more you sit in prayer or meditation before your personal altar, the more the energy itself builds.

The shift in vibration around your altar is strengthened by regular, intentional acts of meditation, prayer, song, chant, and contemplation. If there's no holy inner work going on, the vibration of Spirit won't be present and the portal won't open. It will simply be something pretty to look at, but it won't possess Divine life force. Therefore, I encourage you to create your altar with holy intention, reverence, and enthusiasm.

Some people have questioned whether creating an altar makes a real difference or if it's just for those who are trying to look and feel spiritual when they really don't feel anything at all. My response is that it depends on you. As I mentioned earlier on, spiritual meaning only comes alive with your intention and practice. You can set up an altar, but if it's not invested with meaning through your spiritual intention and regular use, it becomes merely part of the decor.

Long ago, before formal religion took over spirituality, practically everyone had an altar set up at home. Connecting to Divine Source was a very intimate and personal experience all families shared. In ancient times, men and women—and even children—engaged in constant dialogue with their Great Creator. This connection was very personal and wasn't taken for granted. In many parts of the world today, people still have altars in their homes and feel intimately connected with the spirit realm.

We started becoming disconnected from this intimate connection with the spirit realm when our altars were moved out of our homes and into the churches. Bit by bit, we became more removed from a personal relationship with the guiding Spirit within our hearts. Instead, we were misleadingly taught, some even forced to believe, that it was necessary to go through intermediaries such as priests, rabbis, imams, and other clergy members in order to connect with the Divine. Soon enough, and not surprisingly, our personal sensitivity to a higher vibration became dulled and was further diminished by the guilt and shame that was also drilled into us by many religious leaders. This caused the majority of us to nearly totally disconnect from our personal link to Spirit and our Divine Creator, because we were made to feel unworthy. In creating our personal altar we begin to heal these dark feelings of unworthiness lingering in our minds and hearts and reestablish our intimate, loving, personal connection with Spirit once again.

Your connection to your intuition becomes ever more powerful when setting up a beautiful altar that reflects what is sacred to *you*. As you create this sacred portal—your personal place to converse with God, your Higher Self, and your helper guides—you start to regain your confidence, your personal connection to the Divine, and the power that comes with tuning in to your intuition for guidance.

### Where to Place Your Altar

Making room in your home for an altar might not seem like the easiest thing to do, especially if you live in tight quarters, but with a little creativity, it's not difficult. Ideally, you may want to set up your altar in a room that's not used every day, such as a spare bedroom or dining room, or simply clear a small area in any room. A personal altar doesn't require a lot of space—that's not the point. It can be one square foot in size and still open up a tremendous portal if it was created by your heartfelt devotion, love, and intention to connect to your Spirit. I know one woman who shared a two-bedroom apartment with six people, so space was at a premium. She created a small altar on a Kleenex tissue, and no one touched it. If the Spirit is willing, the way is made easy.

My personal altar is in my bedroom. I set it up on a small table in front of the window, and it's one of the first things I see every morning. I love it and always start my day there. It emotes a powerful healing force, enabling me to become grounded and centered on what is important. As I sit at my altar I feel God's love surrounding me. My husband, Patrick, created his own altar in his office on a tall, slim stand. His altar is very different from mine and reflects who he is, which is exactly what it should do. So know that you can certainly have more than one altar in your home. Each family member can set up his or her own unique space—and I believe that everyone should! It's an easy and meaningful way to create a private, sacred portal between you and your Divine Spirit.

### *What to Place on Your Altar*

What you put on your altar is of great importance, as each item must speak directly to a significant part of your inner being and Spirit. Choose whatever energetically resonates with you and touches your heart. For a lot of people, this may mean including a picture of a spiritual figure, such as Mother Mary, Jesus, an Ascended Master Teacher, the Buddha, Krishna, Vishnu, Kali, or the Dalai Lama. Select images or things that really move you in some inner way—those that you feel hold meaning for you at this time. From time to time you may want to change what is on your altar— replacing old items with new ones as your outward life and inner landscape change. The key to creating a powerful altar is *feeling*. So in addition to using images of holy or inspirational figures, also include photos of the people you love, such as your family, friends, and even your pets.

You may also feel inspired to place images and totems from nature, such as seashells, stones, animal bones, or feathers on your altar, as these may carry meaning for your Spirit. You might be drawn to placing beautiful living things on your altar, such as fresh-cut flowers, fresh herbs and spices, or a bowl of clean water that's changed daily to symbolize the holy waters of our loving Mother-Father God, the Source of All Life. Your options are limitless. Be creative, use your imagination, tune in to your intuition, and know that anything goes, as long as it holds meaning for you.

Another way to enhance your altar and make it an ever more powerful one is by adding some natural crystals, especially quartz. Often dismissed by energetically insensitive people as "silly New Age trinkets," crystals are, in fact, extremely powerful living energy tools that can cut negative cords, remove unhealthy energetic attachments, clear energy fields, and amplify your personal intentions. They're essential in many fields today, including technology and medicine; valued for their power and precision; and work with subtle realms of energy in profound ways as well.

That said, don't feel like you have to rush out and get a crystal for your altar just to get one. Wait until such time that a beautiful crystal naturally find its way to you. You may see one in a shop, for example, and feel drawn to it, or a friend may give you one out of the blue as a gift. When something like this happens, it's a clear affirmation from your Spirit that it's listening to you. The more you actively open the door to dialogue with the guiding light within, the more it reaches out to you. So be open, and soon more calling cards from your Spirit will delightfully come your way.

Other wonderful objects to place on your altar are bird feathers, which also seem to somehow suddenly find their way to you once you decide to procure one. Feathers are universal symbols of Spirit and represent the Divine Self in flight. All living things, particularly birds, sense when you're in the process of transformation or elevating your personal vibration as you return to personal power and will show support by offering up their feathers. So pay attention as you move through the day, and don't be surprised if a feather finds you.

Bells, chimes, and rattles are other powerful tools to place on your altar, as they serve to call out to the Divine for guidance and support. Sacred hand drums are also potent tools for connecting with your Spirit and can be placed near your altar for use in connecting with your guiding light. Using these items actually calls your powerful Spirit forward, which is why they've been incorporated into almost all spiritual ceremonies throughout the ages.

While altars are profound gateways to Spirit, they need not be intimidating or overly heavy. To keep my altar's energy light, I like to place a bit of chocolate on it to remind me to remain open to the sweetness of life, no matter how it's unfolding at any given moment. Many ancient religions viewed chocolate as holy, and treasured it for its richness and emotionally soothing qualities. I put a piece of good dark chocolate on my altar as an offering to the Divine Spirit in gratitude for all the sweetness that the benevolent Universe has showered upon me throughout my life. Someone once asked me if I eventually eat the chocolate, but I never do . . . yet interestingly, it always seems to mysteriously disappear.

Beyond these examples, I encourage you to feel free to place anything else on your altar that speaks to your Spirit. And don't hesitate to change or add things to your altar as you move from day to day. An altar is an active, dynamic portal; and as you change and grow, it will, too.

### Approaching Your Altar

Approach your altar as if you were entering a doorway into a sacred space in which you will shift out of ordinary consciousness and into the subtle realm where your Divine Spirit will meet with the heart of God.

Creating a simple ritual to acknowledge this shift of focus is very helpful and invites you into deeper connection with your Divine Spirit and mergence with Source. It may be as simple as lighting a candle or a stick of incense on the altar, or ringing a small bell. It could begin with a small prayer, even a song. As I said, this is your experience and your connection, so you get to create the ritual you want to engage in to activate the sacred portal you are about to enter.

I have a client, for instance, who washes her hands and face before she approaches her altar. To her, this symbolizes purifying her mind and opening up her heart to her Spirit as she temporarily leaves the physical and mental world behind. Another client plays beautiful music beforehand; yet another simply greets her altar each morning with a hearty, "Hello, Father! Hello, Mother!" The ritual is yours to create as part of reclaiming your power. Do what *feels* right to you. Sometimes you might want to approach your altar one way, and on another day your feeling and entire ritual may change. That's okay; it's how your Spirit works as it is the living, breathing, holy essence within you—it's *not* a static or fixed thing. Your Spirit is always ready to communicate with you, so think of this step as a way to open the conversation.

✳

Your personal altar serves as a powerful symbol for the real altar where you meet with your Spirit in your heart space. Envision this space in your heart as the holy foundation of your life—an opening into the unlimited expanse of the Universe. Relax into this heart space. Simply imagine connecting with God. Take your time, and allow whatever thoughts or feelings float freely into your mind. Sit in this space in front of your altar for as long as you can. For the greatest sense of power, you should sit for at least a few minutes every day. If you have more time, do sit longer. Be aware of your breathing, keeping it easy and relaxed. Make sure you don't hold your breath.

If you feel inclined to pray, then do so. If you want to sing, chant, or recite mantras, go ahead and do that. If you need guidance, ask questions. If you aren't self-conscious, ask your questions out loud. Then sit quietly and listen.

If you already have a regular ritual or process that works for you, please continue to use it. If you have a religious practice that feels right to you, please use that. In other words, follow your Spirit, which is the entire point of creating an altar in the first place. Guard against the temptation to believe that there is only one right way to connect to your Divine Self. That kind of thinking is merely a perpetuation of the patriarchal tradition of surrendering power to outside forces. The only way that matters is your way.

Sitting at an altar and entering your heart space daily is the best way to connect with your intuition and the power of your Spirit. Creating an outer altar serves as a means of entering your inner one and facilitates a holy, energetic shift in your life. It's not something that your ego necessarily wants to occur because it will lose power over you, so ignore it if it tries to dismiss your experience as if nothing real is happening.

Tuning in to your guiding Spirit involves dedication, focused intention, constant daily prayer, heightened awareness, regular meditation, and active imagination. If you take the time to formally tune in to your Spirit every day, it eventually becomes automatic. This ritual is richly rewarding and truly strengthens your ability to hear and trust your inner guidance.

### *Harnessing the Power of the Six Directions*

Stand before your altar and visualize yourself floating in the center of an energetic cube in space. See yourself surrounded by the energies and elements of the six directions: East, West, North, South, Above, and Below. Notice that each intersects at a middle point in the center of your heart. They all possess a particular vibration, a unique energetic frequency—a living force, or Spirit— that, if invited and invoked, offers healing and gifts that you can receive in your heart.

Working with the Divine forces of the six directions as you sit at your altar will quickly elevate your sensitivity to the power of your inner guidance. For the remainder of this chapter, I'll describe how to connect to the Spirits of the six directions as my teachers and guides have taught me. Please note that this process may or may not resonate with you, and it shouldn't be considered as the right or only way. I'm just sharing with you what works for me at the moment. I may grow and change over time, and as I do, so will the rituals and techniques that I practice each day.

Now let's move on to some of my suggestions for working with the energies of the six directions of Spirit.

### East

Start by moving your altar so that you're facing eastward as you approach it. If this isn't possible, once you're sitting at your altar, simply turn your body to the East. Focus on this direction, and use your imagination to feel its vibration. The most powerful energy associated with this is, of course, the rising sun. Imagine the sunrise in your mind's eye and feel the vibration it carries with it. If possible, sit at your altar, even if only on occasion, as the sun is rising so that you can directly connect with the sun, the greatest Source of life-force energy for the planet.

The vibration of the East energizes your Spirit with new ideas, inspiration, creative insight, innovation, and opportunities for a fresh start. Turn to the East for these energies to touch, influence, and feed your Spirit. Intuitively open to ways in which your Spirit wants to move into new directions, and allow the frequency and vibration of the East to inform you.

Go even further and appeal to the Spirit of the East for help if you feel that you need a burst of vitality or an infusion of new ideas. Invite the energies of the East in to attract exciting opportunities or experiences if you're in a rut, at a dead end, or at a point in life where you feel uninspired. Then allow yourself to embrace the energetic influence of the East as it touches your heart in service to your Spirit.

## West

Next, focus your attention on the vibration of the West. Feel the energy, frequency, and vibration of what is now behind you and turn around to face it. Imagine the setting sun in your mind's eye as you connect with this powerful living force. Focus on its desire to serve you by pulling away from all energies, activities, or circumstances that no longer serve you or have value in your life. The energy of the West draws all stagnant, dead, or useless vibrations from your energetic field and returns them back to Source. It also assists in releasing grief and sadness from your heart, as these emotions must also eventually be surrendered to the natural flow of life.

Allow yourself to tune in to the living energy of the West by breathing it gently in. Using your intuition, ask yourself what it wants to pull from you. What in your life needs to be finished or completed? In what ways do you need to move on so that you can become present in your life? Don't allow your intellect to interfere with this exploration, as it can't feel the subtle forces of Spirit. That can only be experienced where imagination and wonder rule. Engage your imagination as you invoke the energy of the West to remove all outworn energies so that you can continue to expand your full authentic expression in the natural flow of life.

## North

Next, slowly and with deep breaths and keen awareness, turn your body and attention to the energy of the North. Open your heart up to its powerful vibration. Notice how completely different in feeling and tone this frequency is from that of the East and West, each a unique living conscious force in your life. The energy of the North brings on a cold snap. It wakes your sleeping energy and spurs you into action, helping to get you moving in the direction of your highest purpose in present time.

The energies of the North push you forward in life. This vibration and frequency reveals your next step—your next creation. It urges you to stay in the flow of life and serves as a guiding star of possibility for you to move toward. This is the Spirit of your dreams, your desires, and your intentions. The Spirit of the North reflects back to you who you are naturally designed to be, as the oak tree reflects the potential of the budding acorn. Its energy resonates in your heart to keep you in touch with your soul, which is aching to give birth to greater expression. This powerful force keeps you faithful to your truth, vision, and heart song.

Invoke the energy of the North whenever you feel that you've lost your way. Call upon it when you doubt yourself or feel out of touch with your passion. Allow the energy to touch your heart and pull you back to center—into the flow and aligned with your authentic Self. Let this powerful energy ignite your inner fire and keep you moving forward.

## South

The energy of the South is like a dark cave, symbolizing mystery, wonder, and depth. The energy of kindness, rest, and recuperation, it represents the time for meditation, dreaming, and even slumber. The powerful energy of the South embodies inner knowing and calls upon you to remember who you are. It guides you away from the immediate outer circumstances and leads you into the peaceful, darkened cave within—to a place where thought ceases, feelings quiet, and ancient wisdom speaks.

Invoke the energy of the South when you know it's time to dive deeper into your human journey and capture the more profound meaning of your experiences. Allow its influence to touch your heart and help you feel greater compassion, understanding, and honesty toward yourself. This mysterious force offers you an invitation to return to your original Self. It is the energy of truth. Call upon the energy of the South when you feel you've lost your connection with your true Self and no longer feel your path under your feet. Allow this energy to return you to Self and calm your soul. Seek its power when peace is what you need.

### Above

Maintain your focus, and tune in to the space above you. Feel the vibration of the heavens as you connect with the light above and the stars in the sky. Draw on the power of the subtle Divine beings as they rain their support and wisdom into your crown, the highest point of your head, guiding you on the walk of life.

The energy of the heavens provides companionship, assistance, healing, support, direction, confirmation, and assurance. Make contact with the energy of the heavens for inspiration and to chart your course, stay on the path, and rise to new dimensions. Tune in to its subtle messages—felt in the twinkle of a star, the shifting of the clouds, the hum in your ears, and the love all around you. Open your awareness, and ask the energy of the heavens above to lead your way and keep you true to yourself throughout your journey.

This realm is the playground of the star beings, spirit healers, light beings, angels, and ascended masters. Access their wisdom by directing your attention to the heavens. Feel their presence and follow their loving guidance.

## Below

Continuing to access the Divine flow of all directions, now turn your attention to the energy of the earth. Feel the Great Mother, Gaia, the Divine gorgeous living being who provides the solid foundation beneath your feet. Feel her in your bones, as your physical body is made from her. Open your heart space and let her power move through you. Sense her royalty in nature all around you. Recognize her as a living energy, the most magnificent in the human experience.

Allow your awareness to drift downward deep into the ground. A giant magnetic force is at the center of her core, pulling and keeping the form of the planet together. Feel her heart center pull on your own heart center.

Focus your attention on the countless layers of bones buried in her fields, carrying the presence of your ancestors, as well as all those who have walked the earth before you. Acknowledge that their bones have turned to the dust that now becomes the rich soil for new life and new growth available to you. Tune in to the fullness of her gifts, shared with you in every way. Breathe in her loving Spirit, and be humble before her greatness.

### *Reaching the Heart Space*

Standing in front of your altar, now bring your full awareness and attention inward, to the very center of your heart. This is sacred space, a portal that opens to the unlimited, holy you. It is the point where the Spirits of all six directions converge and commune, coming together in this particular point to assist you in creating your unique life experience.

This is where you leave the three-dimensional physical world and become free to experience your unlimited, authentic Spirit. As you enter the heart space, you cease to be contained by linear time or space, by your history or family, or by past or present circumstances. All of this fades away. It is your experience, but not your true Self.

While gently breathing, focus your attention on journeying even deeper into your heart space. With each inward breath, envision going around and around as if you were a stream of water swirling down a drain. With your inner eye, watch your awareness travel in this manner until it finally drops into the very center of your heart and opens into an infinite, unlimited world on the other side.

Don't worry if this expanded sense of being doesn't occur the first time you try to enter your heart space. Simply focus on the center of your heart and let yourself experience whatever awareness comes about. Sit quietly in that space for a few minutes, remembering to relax, breathe, and listen.

☀

It's highly likely that when beginning to tune in to the realm of Spirit—especially if this is a new practice—you may feel very little or nothing at all. Don't let that frustrate you. In working with an altar, you'll soon awaken to the more subtle perceptions, although they may be barely noticeable at first. Be patient. Believe that your Spirit is listening and will connect with you, and it will happen. You determine the rate of progress by your own level of consistency and devotion.

I suggest that you view this entire project—creating and sitting at your altar—as something you truly love and enjoy. At the very least, your altar will become a place where you can quietly gather your thoughts, calm your mind, pray, and meditate. At best, your heart will open and you'll experience a profound direct connection with your powerful guiding Spirit that will alter your life completely.

If you spend time at your altar every day as part of your spiritual practice, you'll establish such a powerful connection to your Spirit that you'll actually be able to feel its higher, more peaceful vibration the minute you enter its energetic field. Soon the same sense of peace will become a part of your energetic field that you carry forward into your day. The beautiful energy you create when you're meditating there draws you into your Spirit gently and easily.

You'll soon find yourself looking forward to sitting at your altar each morning. Since it serves as your meeting place with Spirit, maintaining contact with your Divine authentic Self no longer seems so challenging. You have successfully begun the journey through the first two steps, awakening to and slowly discovering your inner voice, your inner power, your guiding Spirit. You're putting forth the effort by incorporating what you're learning into your daily life. Thus, the creation of your own altar serves as a natural springboard to the third step of personal empowerment: *taking the leap* and surrendering to your Spirit.

# Chapter Five

# STEP THREE:
# TAKING THE LEAP

The next step toward living a life of deep satisfaction and meaningful purpose is actually taking the leap and following your intuition wherever it may lead and not thinking about it anymore. This means moving beyond the parameters and perceived safety of your ego and relying on the mysterious, unlimited power of your inner voice for guidance. Taking the leap by fully trusting your Spirit to lead you in life at first feels as though you're jumping off a cliff, when you're actually surrendering your ego over to a higher wisdom, which actually lays a more solid foundation of truth under your feet.

Surrendering to your inner guidance means recognizing that your ego has highly limited, if any, real power, and is preventing you from feeling at peace or realizing your potential. While discovering your inner voice is exciting, until you surrender to it and allow it to take the lead in your life, what you discover won't make any practical difference. You'll remain trapped, struggling to stay a step ahead of your fears.

Surrendering to your Spirit may be too great to fathom at first, and it can feel as if you're being asked to take a crazy leap into the abyss. It is a leap . . . but not into the abyss. You're stepping into the flow of life and the full support of the Universe. When you surrender your ego and trust your inner guidance, you come to realize that what your ego knows is not *all* there is to know, what your ego perceives is not necessarily an accurate view of the world, and what your ego thinks is possible is not *all* that is truly possible. So you open to the Universe and ask it to show you another, better way to live.

For some, taking this leap feels like death to the ego. It isn't. Rather, it's more like a demotion. As I've said earlier, the rational mind by itself isn't really the problem. However, depending on the intellect to do a job that it's inherently not equipped and qualified to do is the *real* problem. The rational mind, or shielding ego, is a biased, limited apparatus that seeks solutions from a defensive and distorted point of view, generally leading you down the wrong road. Your inner guidance, your Spirit, on the other hand, allows you direct access to the quantum field of all possibility. It is by tuning in to your inner guidance that the most loving solutions, inspired insights, and profound personal healings are revealed. To take the leap means to let go of control, get out of your own way, and have faith in your inner voice, your authentic Self. The faster you put two feet in and go with the guidance of your Spirit, the faster the world stops feeling threatening and you start feeling better.

Rarely does giving up resistance and giving over to your Spirit happen with a single decision, moment, or event. Even if you are fully willing to take the leap and trust your intuition, you still have to break free of the bad habits of living from the ego mind-set you've been taught. Fully abandoning yourself to your inner guidance takes both your conscious intention and strong, consistent practice. After all, the ego doesn't give up its power easily and loves to put up a fight.

Realistically, surrendering to your inner voice happens one step at a time, one choice at a time. Consciously making the choice to listen to your vibes every day in small, nonthreatening ways is best. For example, if your inner guidance suggests you leave early for work, do it. If your inner guidance suggests taking a different direction home from work, do it. If it suggests you call your mother and check on her, once again, do it. Each time you say yes to your inner guidance, you take another step toward building the kind of trust that only comes from experience, the kind of trust that complete surrender demands. It may take weeks, months, or even years before your ego truly gives up and trusts your Spirit, but if you keep taking small steps in that direction, the huge leap you think you must make never quite appears. Stepping more and more into a Spirit-guided life in little ways makes it easier and easier to do, and before you know it, you've made the leap you feared. Because you will have such positive experiences each time you choose to follow your inner guidance, it will become more and more compelling to continue.

Opportunities to loosen the ego's grip on you present themselves in many ways, both small and large, throughout each day. Your task is to grab them. Every time you go with the flow of your intuitive impulses, the outcome will be so positive, so surprising, and so much better than your ego could have ever created on its own that before you know it, it will become obvious that trusting your inner voice is the only sane way to live.

How difficult this is will be up to you. Surrendering ego control can be a gradual transfer of power or an intense battle. Either way, in the end your ego will never prevail over your Spirit in guiding you back to integrity with your true Self.

### *Playing the Tabla*

Perhaps the biggest leap we must make when tuning back in to our intuition and following our Spirit is that of leaving the old, the familiar, and the comfortable and becoming a willing beginner, open and available to learning something brand new.

I have a friend named Ben who is a wonderful drummer and has been playing for more than 20 years. He said his skills came naturally to him and required no real thought or awareness on his part. He just feels the music and bangs away to the rhythm. Over the years, he's played with several bands and his talent has grown, yet he's never recalled a time when he had to really focus or work at it. It's just what he did.

Then Ben went to India, where he experienced masterful Indian musicians playing an ancient type of drums called the *tabla* (a pair of hand drums that are of different sizes and produce different timbres), and he was so moved by the performance that it nearly brought him to tears. He was mesmerized and entered a deep trancelike state. It was unlike any other musical experience he'd ever had, either while playing or listening.

The tabla spoke to his soul and awoke something in him. It felt like coming home. Immediately, he knew he wanted to create that music for himself. So when Ben returned to Chicago, he bought a beautiful pair of tabla at a world-music store and sat down to play them as soon as he got home. However, no matter what he tried, he couldn't re-create the sounds that the Indian musicians had made. Every single thing he knew about drumming—every natural impulse, every learned technique—completely failed to bring forth any semblance of music out of these strange drums. The way he was used to playing simply didn't work (and he could play many different types of percussion instruments).

For the first time, Ben couldn't wing it, nor could he fake it. He couldn't even teach himself to play these drums, as he'd done many times in the past. They seemed to have a different set of rules, and he had no idea what they were. He didn't know where to begin. The tabla spoke a completely foreign language.

Ben was shocked and frustrated by this unexpected barrier. He hadn't planned on this requiring much effort on his part, and he certainly didn't think the possibility existed that he wouldn't be able to play them at all.

He realized that if he wanted to play this instrument, he'd have to start all over. He would have to become a beginner, which meant unlearning everything he already knew about percussion. This challenged his ego significantly. He'd even have to find a teacher and make time to practice. But he was already so busy. It seemed like a lot more work than it was worth, so he walked away for a while and let the drums sit in the corner, silent.

After nine months of ignoring (or at least attempting to ignore) the tabla, Ben's ego quieted down enough for him to once again feel his Spirit urging him to play them. He knew that it was his ego stopping him from engaging in the experience that was calling to him now. He didn't want to be a beginner, a student. He certainly didn't want someone to show him how to do something that he already knew how to do. *I'm a good drummer,* he'd say to himself. *Why should I stress myself out trying to learn this? I won't use the tabla anyway. I have no place to play them. What's the point?* And so the conversation went in his head . . . yet as convincing as it was, it never felt true. His desire to play didn't go away; his ego just overwhelmed and silenced it.

Then one day, after Ben enjoyed an unusually peaceful morning, he looked up from his computer and the tabla seemed to wink at him. It was as if they were trying to tell him something: *Come on, Ben. It's time to learn. Don't be afraid. Open your heart and mind, and enter the unknown.*

Suddenly, all of his excuses faded away. Something in him opened up. He felt ready! His ego was finally quiet, and he could hear the Spirit of the tabla calling to him, just as it had the first time he'd heard it in India. In that moment, he surrendered and said *yes.* He stopped avoiding what his heart yearned for, and instead decided to move toward it. What did he have to lose?

Ben found a great teacher—one of the best in the world, in fact—and began the arduous learning process. It has been going very slowly for him and each lesson challenges his patience, dedication, and ego in every way. On some days, he practices making a single sound, over and over again, for 45 minutes or more. Just one sound. His lessons require that he be mindful of everything he does with his hands and fingers, from where he places them on the drums to how hard he must flick his wrist to produce a particular tone. Nothing about this process is automatic, at least not yet. It takes great focus, awareness, and intention on his part to succeed in the tiniest way. There are still days when he wonders why he's bothering to do this.

But he *is* bothering. He's inspired by training his mind to work in new ways. And each victorious note he creates on the tabla, however small, feels like he just won a gold medal. Most of all, his effort brings his Spirit tremendous satisfaction. The more he surrenders his ego to his intention, the more vibrant and joyful he feels—not just about the tabla, but about every aspect of his life.

When he's practicing, Ben stops thinking and simply experiences the instrument. His mind becomes quiet. The past and future go away, and he feels timeless. His discipline rewards him with soul satisfaction, giving voice to his evolving Spirit. These kinds of benefits can't be measured in the physical, ego-based world. Ben isn't able to play well enough for others yet, and he's a long way from being able to make money playing the tabla at his current skill level. If anything, he'd be met with wrinkled brows and curious remarks. His effort is strictly personal, and the rewards are, too.

That is exactly why this process is so worthwhile. Ben is doing what his Spirit wants for himself, not anyone else, and he's putting forth the discipline and effort it commands in spite of his ego-based objections. His ego doesn't want to relinquish its power, so it still constantly urges him to quit. Yet since he made the choice to act on his Spirit's desire, his ego's efforts to distract him have become weak and ineffectual, and are surprisingly easy to ignore.

In following his Spirit, Ben is challenged and fed by his experience. When he's working on his daily lessons, he feels present and fully alive. The rest of the world fades away; all that remains is his intention, his Spirit, the Spirit of the tabla, and the Spirit of music. He is discovering that they're all expressions of the same thing, which is love. Without his concerted effort, he wouldn't have had this profound, expansive awareness of himself and life.

### Tuning In

Tuning in and living an intuitively guided, Spirit-based life takes attention, discipline, effort, and practice. More often than not, what comes easily or even feels "natural" to you isn't in alignment with your authentic Self. To shift from ego to Spirit requires a big change in your life—changing your priorities and values, how you spend your time, your inner dialogue, your focus, your availability to others, and your ability to surrender control. This is where the effort on your part comes in.

Consider this: Making the leap from living according to your ego to living according your Spirit is like learning to play a new game, with all new rules for being successful. The rules of the ego-based world start with: "Live for others' approval." The Spirit-guided rules start with: "Live for your own approval, and be willing to stand in the discomfort of others' disapproval if necessary." The ego-based rules continue with: "Don't change anything; it's dangerous." The Spirit-guided rule is: "Embrace change. Welcome it. It's natural and healthy, and it brings growth." The ego-based rule is: "Be responsible and do your duty. If what you're doing doesn't make money or serve a practical purpose, then it's a waste of time." The Spirit-guided rule is: "If it calls to you, speaks to your creativity, brings out your most authentic Self, honors your truth, opens your heart, and challenges you to grow, then it is important and responsible to explore."

The ego wants things to be controllable, predictable, and easy. If change is involved, the ego will do everything to stop it. To the ego, change means danger or even death. The rational mind relies on the past to guide it in the moment, and change signifies that the past doesn't apply now. The paradox is that once you begin to tune in and take the leap to follow your inner guidance, you become more creative, more solution-oriented, more relaxed and at ease. Surprisingly, your ego quiets down. It resists change until it is happening. Then the resistance stops, and your Spirit takes over.

## Asking the Questions

Close your eyes and calmly breathe in and out through your nose. Start with a sigh or two to help you relax. Massage your jaw and throat a little to release even more tension and fear held in that part of your body, your expression center. Feel the energetic tension that your racing mind creates in your body. Do you notice how it drains your energy, your life force, your kefi, right out of you?

Now relax the tension in your neck and throat as much as possible with a few gentle stretches and take in a deep, easy, belly-filling breath. Don't force your breath to enter your body by raising your shoulders and holding your head back. Rather, keep your shoulders comfortably relaxed and down, and allow your belly to pull the air in naturally without any tension at all. Exhale by releasing the sound "Ah," and then bring the corners of your lips up to your ears in a gentle smile.

Next, take out your journal and tune inward. Contemplate each of the following questions and invite your inner guidance—your Spirit—to respond to each one. Give yourself plenty of time to feel the genuine response coming from your heart, the source of your true power.

- What new creative expression or learning experience is calling to you? For example, playing a new instrument, taking voice lessons, signing up for a painting class, making time for a spiritual retreat, learning a new language, going rock climbing, enrolling in a digital-photography course, or writing poetry?

- How long have you felt this impulse or urging? A week, month, or even years? Where do you think this is coming from?

- Are you listening to this impulse and following it? If you are, what challenges has this brought up?

- What rewards are you experiencing by surrendering to your inner urgings?

- How does it feel to open up to exploring new avenues, places, people, things, and even parts of your own nature?

- If you aren't following these impulses from your Spirit, what are the reasons you give yourself for not doing so? Do they feel true?

- How afraid are you to explore or experiment with new things or direction? What scares you the most?

- How does it feel to try to prevent things from changing? (Try to be as specific as possible.)

- How does your choice to say *no* to your inner voice leave you feeling? Energized? Constrained? (Again, be as specific as possible.)

- Do you wonder what saying *yes* to the urgings of your Spirit might do for you? Do you allow yourself to contemplate such things?

After writing down your answers, set aside your journal and remain seated. Close your eyes and calmly breathe in and out through your nose. Start with a sigh or two to help you relax. Quiet your mind and listen. What is your Spirit urging or encouraging you to do? Are you willing to give it a try?

With your next breath, let all of your tension go and simply *be* for a moment or two, even longer if possible. Enjoy sitting and breathing deeply, empty of all thought, free of any agenda, centered in the moment. Feel this vibration of being connected to Source. Notice how peaceful, content, and even energized you feel. This is the power of your Spirit, and it's available to you at all times. It is the real you. *Remember this.*

### Daily Ritual: Say "Yes" to Your Spirit

Choose to follow one creative impulse or urge arising from your Spirit every day, the simpler the better. It could be as basic as doodling in a sketchbook for five minutes every day or as ambitious as signing up for a foreign-language class that meets regularly. Since this involves introducing something new into your life, trade it for one habit or practice that you do now but doesn't add genuine value or joy to your Spirit at this time.

For example, you may be in the habit of watching the news every evening, yet doing so leaves you distraught and anxious. You can quit watching the news and practice playing the piano instead. Or perhaps you have the habit of going online every day, checking your Facebook page or surfing the Internet with no particular destination in mind after checking e-mail; and yet it consumes 20 to 40 minutes every day (if not more). Exchange the bulk of your time spent online for a creative effort such as painting with watercolors, woodworking, drawing, learning to make a new recipe, or practicing your French lessons.

It may seem impossible to find the time, and your ego will certainly object, but do it anyway. Resist your ego's objections, and go for the experience your Spirit is requesting with as little negative self-talk as possible. Be prepared for the potential sabotage from others you may encounter, and ready yourself for it. For example, just as you sit down at the piano, your five-year-old starts fighting with his sibling. Before jumping up, see if they can work it out. You may be just starting to write in your journal when the phone rings. Instead of leaping up to answer it, allow the caller to leave a message and continue focusing on your priority. Don't waste energy fighting distractions; just ignore them. Following your Spirit is worth the initial challenge. Try it for a week and see how well you succeed. Above all, notice how tuning in and saying yes to your inner voice rather than your ego makes you feel.

### Secret Death Wish

When our Spirit calls out, we must eventually leap into the unknown if we are to follow it and return to our authentic Self. Once the call is made, it becomes increasingly difficult to ignore it or run away from it in fear, though we may try. Eventually we must all turn inward and come face-to-face with our true inner Self.

Eric had always been known as a great guy. Everyone loved him. If anyone, anywhere, had a problem, he was immediately on hand to help. People admired and respected him throughout the small town where he lived. No one suspected he had a secret. They couldn't. What would they think? It would ruin everything. So for years, he didn't admit it—not even to himself.

Eric married Jeanne, his high-school sweetheart, 26 years ago. Now, four beautiful daughters later, he was silently suffering from a deep, immovable depression. He endured what he felt had become a sterile, soul-deadening, sexless marriage for a long time. He didn't blame his wife for the way things had deteriorated between them. If anything, he blamed himself.

On paper, Jeanne was the best partner a person could have. The house was impeccable, and she took care of their daughters like a CEO overseeing a beloved business. Everything was well managed and their children were supported in every way. From schoolwork and school clothes, to extracurricular activities and Girl Scouts meetings, Jeanne handled it all like a champ. Eric was grateful not to have to deal with any of it. He believed he wouldn't know how to and regarded his wife as the maestro of all things domestic. He just couldn't figure out when their relationship had gotten so lost—and truthfully, he wasn't sure if he wanted to find it again.

Eric's job was another source of quiet despair. He had a sign business that he'd inherited from his father. It was profitable, and he appreciated his loyal employees. It wasn't that stressful either. It's just that he really hated it. But he felt badly for feeling that way, and he definitely wouldn't admit how he felt. Many people, especially his family, reminded him all too often how he ought to be grateful to have a reliable income, particularly when so many others were out of work. Furthermore, the business enabled him to be a good provider, which he prided himself on.

Between his empty marriage and unfulfilling job, Eric's life became more and more depressing. He often avoided his work and procrastinated on things he had to do at home. Then he'd go in the opposite direction and throw himself into his mounting responsibilities in an attempt to make up for the time he had wasted. No matter how he reasoned it or how hard he tried to deny it, he felt trapped. But he wouldn't let himself think about it too much. It was his duty to carry on. He was, after all, responsible. And yet, the older his daughters became, the more he struggled with why he had to be so responsible.

He left or, more accurately, ran away from his home life every chance he got, engaging in risky, high-adrenaline sports, such as rock climbing, downhill ski racing, or high-speed motorcycle rides on steep country hills. He'd do anything to quell the frustration and anger that was boiling inside him. And as he tried to outrun his dissatisfaction, he wondered how he could feel so wrong in spite of his efforts to do things so "right"—at least according to the rules he was given by his parents, church, and whomever else. They were just implied, and so he complied.

One day Eric had a disastrous accident. While riding his motorcycle with a friend at lightning speed down a dirt road, his front wheel was punctured on an unexpected rock and exploded, throwing him 50 feet into the air. He landed headfirst and on his shoulder. The blow caused a main artery in his neck to burst.

*This is it,* he thought, almost relieved, as he lay on the ground bleeding. *I'm going to die.* Soon after, he vaguely remembered being airlifted out of the valley and flown to a nearby hospital. He missed the rest and slipped into unconsciousness.

Eric didn't die, although according to his doctors, he should have. Instead, he was miraculously pieced back together and returned to the life he secretly wished to exit. That's when his greatest pain settled in. He could no longer run from his misery as he had tried to before. He couldn't even walk away from it now. He could only lie in bed and think about his life—or take lots of painkillers to forget about it, but they made him extremely nauseated so that wasn't really an option. He had to face his feelings, and that scared him more than anything.

Eric's body recovered over time, but his inner struggle continued. Having to slow down, even stop, and be forced to think about his present situation all day long was excruciatingly difficult. Then one day in the waiting room at the rehabilitation center where he was receiving weekly physical-therapy treatments, he overheard a conversation between two women about the idea of a person's Spirit. It was subtle, yet strong enough to make him notice. He wasn't even sure what the word meant exactly, so he Googled it and learned that it's from the Latin *spiritus,* or "breath," and refers to the noncorporeal body of a human.

*The "noncorporeal"—the part that's not my skin and bones. Not even the brain matter in my head,* he thought. *Interesting. No one in my life has ever talked about that. . . .*

The minute Eric opened the door to Spirit, something inside him woke up. He instinctively knew what it was. It was the feeling he had been running from all these years. It was his Spirit that had been chasing him, trying to get his attention. And to his surprise, it was his own authentic Self that he had been afraid of.

His cloud of depression eased a little and was replaced by overwhelming curiosity. Like a detective who has discovered a key to a secret treasure chest, he followed the trail and decided to explore. He began to ask himself how he truthfully felt about his life and allowed his heart to respond over his intellect. He expected silence, but was surprised that as soon as he asked, his Spirit was waiting to respond. Eric took a deep breath, and for the first time in years, actually made contact in his heart space. It felt real and genuine, and thankfully, very good.

*Why am I so afraid of my Spirit?* he wondered for days and weeks afterward. Bit by bit, the answer revealed itself. It was because his Spirit revealed the truth that his life was artificial. The person he carried himself as in the world—the one everyone loved and applauded—wasn't who he really was inside. He was an actor, a fake. He realized that he'd given up his true nature long ago in order to please others.

Eric tuned even more deeply in to his heart by meditating, practicing basic yoga, slowing down, and taking recuperative walks. As he did so, he talked with his Spirit out loud and listened intently for clues, for any guidance on how to feel better. In time, his Spirit showed him how most of his actions were done automatically—without thinking (or even wanting to think), and most of all, without any regard for himself. It was almost as if he were playing the part of a superhero with a magic cape that he'd put on the minute there was a call for help. He liked the attention in the beginning because it made him feel special and important. But now he only felt suffocated and trapped by his persona.

Through his Spirit, Eric intuited that he had shut out his wife because he didn't like feeling close to her. It made him feel scared and vulnerable. They were like actors in a play called "Married Life," and when the play went from that to "Family Life," he lost the starring role. He found himself in the background, and it wasn't fun or fulfilling—at least not in the way he decided to play his part.

The more he tuned in to and listened to his Spirit, the more scared yet relieved he became. He was afraid because he knew he couldn't continue living a lie, but he also didn't know how to undo what seemed so set in stone. The relief he experienced was because at least now he felt authentic and didn't have to hide his secret, at least not from himself.

Several times he wanted to deny everything and go back to the miserable, unconscious life he had lived before his accident. Yet he knew he couldn't. He was a dead man in that life. The accident was just his way to confirm this truth to others. As hard as it was to look at the mountainous mess he needed to extricate himself from—and face the upset it would cause the people he loved—he knew he had to begin for his Spirit's sake. His world was imploding anyway. At least he felt a genuine heartbeat of excitement for the first time in a long, long while.

Once Eric connected to his Spirit, he couldn't keep his secret from others much longer. One by one, starting with his wife, he told everyone the truth. He explained that he wanted—no, he *needed*—a different life, a different job, and a different kind of personal relationship. He craved a different identity, one that wasn't trapped by feeding off the approval of others.

What happened after his confession surprised him. He expected a catastrophic reaction—sure that his revelation would destroy his wife, shock his friends, hurt his children, ruin his reputation, and embarrass his parents. But none of his fears were realized. Everyone just listened to what he had to say and told him that they had known all along: "We just want you to be happy. Please do what you have to do for all of our sakes!"

And so Eric's second life began. He threw away his Superman cape—mentally, that is. He kept his sign business going but also took up woodworking, which he loved, so his job wasn't defining him anymore. He moved out of his home and into a small studio apartment. It was simple: just a bed, a lamp, and a refrigerator. But it was *his* space, and he loved it. He started experimenting with his look and wearing different clothes. He even grew a ponytail for a while, but eventually cut it off because it didn't feel right. But it did feel right to try.

The most interesting part of Eric's journey is that on some level, everyone in his life has been affected by his shift back to a more authentic Self. They are curiously watching and learning. As upsetting as it has been to the status quo, Eric's decision to take the leap and follow his heart and intuition feels right to all of them. It benefits them, too.

Outwardly, Eric's life is still quite a mess—but it's an exciting, evolving, authentic mess. His children, now young adults, are accepting his changes and asking him a lot of questions. He is finally speaking to them on a genuine, heartfelt level, and they're starting to really get to know each other for the first time. His wife isn't happy that he's living in a studio so that he can find himself, but she isn't totally shattered. She, too, has been positively influenced, even if it wasn't something she sought out or even wanted. She's asking the same questions of herself that Eric began asking after his accident. That's how the Spirit works: As one person wakes up, he or she awakens another and another and so on. The day will eventually come when all of us will be awake.

Eric and his wife aren't sure about the future of their marriage. They know that they love something inside each other, but they have to find it in themselves first. This is the only way *real* love is possible, and finding that real love is what letting the Spirit lead is all about.

### Tuning In

When taking the leap and surrendering to your Spirit, you must tune in to your heart and admit how you feel, first to yourself and then to others—even if your truth makes you or those around you uncomfortable, unhappy, angry, hurt, or afraid. Admitting your true feelings makes you vulnerable, so the ego tries to keep you from doing this at all costs. But it's only when you accept your vulnerability and surrender ego control that you can follow your powerful Spirit. It's the only way to truly ground your life in authenticity.

Wrestling control away from your ego and giving it over to the greater guidance of your Spirit necessitates change in many or, perhaps, most aspects of your life. This can be scary, so once again, your ego will try to distract you, stop you, and convince you to suppress the truth. This doesn't work, however, as your inner voice, once awakened, will not be silenced for long. You might temporarily ignore or bury your feelings, but they will never completely go away. Instead, they turn into anger, depression, irritability, and sadness.

It can be scary to look at your life and admit that it isn't working or doesn't feel authentic. To surrender to your Spirit is to live your truth and build your life upon that truth. Trying to hold an artificial existence together indefinitely is futile and will leave you feeling drained and miserable. And you aren't kidding anyone—others feel your unhappiness. Remember that your unlimited creative power is available to you and all those who could benefit from it as soon as you surrender control and follow your intuition to a more authentic existence.

### Asking the Questions

Close your eyes and calmly breathe in and out through your nose. Start with a sigh or two to help you relax. Massage your jaw and throat a little to release even more tension and fear held in that part of your body, your expression center. Feel the energetic tension that your racing mind creates in your body. Do you notice how it drains your energy, your life force, your kefi, right out of you?

Now relax the tension in your neck and throat as much as possible with a few gentle stretches and take in a deep, easy, belly-filling breath. Don't force your breath to enter your body by raising your shoulders and holding your head back. Rather, keep your shoulders comfortably relaxed and down, and allow your belly to pull the air in naturally without any tension at all. Exhale by releasing the sound "Ah," and then bring the corners of your lips up to your ears in a gentle smile.

Next, take out your journal and turn your attention inward. Contemplate each of the following questions and invite your Spirit, your most authentic Self, to respond to each one. Give yourself plenty of time to feel the genuine response coming from your heart, the source of your true power.

- Where in your life is your Spirit expressing dissatisfaction or unhappiness? Be specific.

- In what ways are you feeling out of touch with your inner truth? Why do you think this is so?

- Are you keeping a secret or running away from your Spirit?

- Are you afraid of initiating the changes that your inner voice is now urging you to make?

- Are you fearful of being authentic with the people in your life? If so, what do you think will happen if you surrender to your Spirit?

- What do you fear most? Whom do you fear most? What do you internally struggle with? Explain in detail.

- What does your ego hold on to? Are there aspects of yourself or your life that no longer feel authentic? How does that make you feel?

- If you were to admit to yourself and the world what your Spirit longs for right now, what would it be? Have you surrendered to your inner truth, or are you trying to ignore it? Be honest.

- How do you feel after answering these questions? Tune in to your heart, and take your time before answering. Relax and listen. Don't rush.

After writing down your answers, set aside your journal and remain seated. Close your eyes and calmly breathe in and out through your nose. Start with a sigh or two to help you relax. Tune in to your Spirit. If you could change something in your life, what would it be? What is your heart telling you?

With your next breath, let all of your tension go and simply *be* for a moment or two, even longer if possible. Enjoy sitting and breathing deeply, empty of all thought, free of any agenda, centered in the moment. Feel this vibration of being in touch with your intuition and Spirit. Notice how peaceful, content, and even energized you feel. There is power in your Spirit, and it's available to you at all times. It is the real you. *Remember this.*

### Daily Ritual: Speak from Your Heart

Before you speak, take a deep breath and tune in to your heart and Spirit, and speak from there, even if it frightens you. This may first involve facing your deepest feelings, especially if you've been inauthentic all of your life.

Start by saying the following sentence out loud, every day: "If I weren't afraid, I would . . . " and then complete the statement. Continue speaking out loud for two to three minutes. If possible, do this first thing in the morning when you're sitting at your altar. At least make some time each day to do this when you won't be interrupted or distracted.

Listen to your responses and feel the energy they unleash within you. Compare what your Spirit longs for to your present situation. Where is the disparity? How big a disparity is it? Is the life you're presently living somewhat near the life you long for? Are parts of it exactly as you want them to be? What parts aren't? Tune in to the energy of those parts of your life that you don't want. How would you describe the feelings that arise? Do you feel restless, agitated, hopeless, afraid, hurt, trapped, or dead? Now feel the energy in your heart when focused on the life you envision. How would you describe this energy? Do you feel more relaxed, more peaceful? Are you suddenly more confident and satisfied? Today, take one step in the direction your Spirit longs for.

If you want a different job, begin the process of looking for one. If you want to work for yourself, write down your ideal job description. If you crave time alone, make the decision to take it in small increments and mark it on your calendar. If you want a change, tell the people it would most affect that you're intending to make some shifts in your life and need their support. Be calm and don't ask for permission when sharing your truth. Be kind and compassionate, and have respect for others' reactions. Change scares everyone and can bring up the fear of abandonment. Simply explain that you've abandoned yourself and must return to your inner truth before you can be genuinely and fully present in the best possible way to others. Ask the people in your life for their love and understanding. Don't expect them to agree with what you're doing—they may not, and that is their right.

Follow your intuition and Spirit regardless of the circumstances. Invite others to explore their inner truth with you, but don't insist. Choosing to tune in and listen to your intuition is a personal calling and comes to each of us in the right time. You cannot force this desire on someone else, so don't try to. Listen to others' fears if they react, but don't defend your intention. You have the right and the need to follow your intuition, be authentic, and live your highest truth. The Universe requires that of all of us sooner or later. Taking the leap to follow your intuition over your fears liberates and serves everyone in the end, even if it's a disruptive, messy process along the way. Be loving *and* courageous.

Every single day, take one definitive step in the direction of your authentic Self. If you're afraid to follow your intuition, admit it, but take that one step anyway. As you do, notice how the Universe meets you halfway. Pay attention to how you feel as you choose to allow your Spirit to lead your life as opposed to being led by your fears.

As you continue to follow your Spirit, notice how your body feels, how you sleep, how you breathe, and even how your heart feels. How does the world around you feel? Write this down in your journal. Like undertaking a grand experiment, it's vital to take action in support of your intuition every day, even if it's just baby steps, and be aware of the changes these actions brings about if you want to get into flow with your highest Self. Let your experience be your guide—not your thoughts or fears. Breathe and do, one day at a time. Eventually, you'll see that the more you listen to your inner voice and follow it, the more your mind quiets down and stays calm. Congratulate yourself when this occurs, because it means you're in the process of a great and powerful transformation.

### The Raging Battle

Taking the leap toward living an intuitively charted life requires trust. You must learn to trust not only your heart, but also to trust others. Once you begin to follow your intuition, you cannot help but notice how you are *not* alone, that your actions invariably affect others. Sometimes, your actions inspire others to help you, and it's important to be open and not to resist or reject their assistance. Taking the leap can mean leaping into an armchair, where you give up control, rest, and allow others to step in and support you.

On the surface, Barbara had everything under control. She was a successful orthopedic surgeon who had built up a significant clientele over the years. She had been married to a decent man for more than 30 years; and together they raised two responsible sons, who were both currently enrolled in medical school at highly prestigious universities. She was extremely proud of her children.

Barbara, with some help from her husband, had paid off their home, amassed a solid retirement account, and in addition to financing her sons' education (which was considerable), also managed to pay all the bills without too much trouble. She definitely ran a tight ship and felt that she did a good job. Yet, in spite of all these positive accomplishments, she often felt frustrated and unhappy—a fact that she couldn't hide very well.

To make matters worse, she was ashamed of her chronically petulant state of mind and would chastise herself because other people suffered with "real" problems and challenges. This thinking only made her feel even more guilty and angry with herself for not being at peace. In an attempt to relax, she consulted a psychotherapist, who, after many sessions, suggested that her mental state might be rooted in a chemical imbalance. Thus, her therapist prescribed an anti-anxiety medication to assist in balancing and calming her moods. Open to trying anything that might help her step out from under the persistent storm cloud she was under, she agreed. But even that failed to make a difference. After six months on the medication, she didn't feel any better—in fact, her agitation grew worse.

From time to time, Barbara tried to justify her sour outlook by finding things around her to blame it on. Yet deep down, she knew those things weren't the issue. Her agitation signified something else: her Spirit was angry, and she could no longer deny it.

Barbara's Spirit announced itself everywhere. It spoke through her increased impatient outbursts with her staff and even her patients. It spoke when she would go straight to her bedroom once she got home after work, declining all social invitations and asking to be left alone.

Barbara knew this internal battle had to stop, and so did everyone else. Thankfully, her family stepped up to the plate. Due to her increasingly "crazy" behavior, they had an intervention of sorts and insisted that she take time off from her responsibilities and rest. Secretly, she was relieved. She wanted to surrender to her Spirit and give up control, but she was deathly afraid of the consequences. When her family demanded that she stop and take care of herself, it was as if a Divine force had stepped in and given her the permission she needed.

Barbara turned her practice over to a trusted colleague and went on an indefinite sabbatical. It took her nearly three months to regain enough energy to even begin to listen to her inner voice, but she was on her way. Bit by bit, she made progress. Slowly, as Barbara surrendered more and more to her inner guidance, she rediscovered what joy and pleasure felt like. Relief came in small surges as she allowed Divine support to flow in.

She started to recognize what filled her up and also what drained her. To her surprise, she discovered that much of what had made up her life before her "breakdown" was fulfilling and meaningful. She loved being a doctor and helping others. It just couldn't be a one-way street of willful over-giving anymore.

She realized that life wasn't something she had to fearfully control. It was something to allow and experience, to learn from and enjoy; her Spirit was frustrated with her for refusing this gift. Her unhappy, angry state was an honest reflection of her willful self-neglect and rejection of the goodness of life. Now that the internal fire of her Spirit's anger was doused, she understood the futility of pretending that she was, or could be, in charge of everything at all times.

She finally took the leap and decided to let her Spirit be her guide. Barbara returned to work, but she cut down her hours significantly. She and her husband sold their expensive home and bought a townhouse closer to the office. She planted her first garden in their small backyard. Putting her hands in the ground cooled her agitation like no medication ever could. In the rich earth, she found a source of energy that gave her something that rejuvenated her soul—and she couldn't get enough. Gardening became her passion, her play, her meditation, and her prayer. She felt in direct contact with God and with her true Self when she was alone with her plants.

Tending to her garden taught her how to surrender control over things. While she was the one who planted and cared for her plants, she didn't cause the seeds to grow. In admitting this, she learned to respect and trust the Divine forces greater than her own ego. This calmed her fears and allowed her to quit trying to save the world. It didn't need saving. She was part of it—she didn't need to run it.

Barbara marveled at the intensity with which she had resisted her inner guidance for so long. It wasn't as if she were ever truly confused about what she needed to do to feel whole and peaceful. Intuitively, she knew. In retrospect, she realized that it was because she confused surrender with submission, and she didn't want to lose herself any more than she already had.

On the other side of her transformation, living at peace with her Spirit, she discovered that to surrender means to allow something greater to take over and nourish her—not strangle her as her ego had feared. When she let go and trusted her intuition, her Spirit led her to a much simpler, more internally spacious life. This is what she had secretly desired all along, but couldn't see a way to make possible. It wasn't until she took the leap to trust her intuition and go with it that the solutions and support showed up. And to her great surprise, nothing collapsed—another illusion of her ego lifted. In fact, her orthopedic practice remained quite stable and not one patient left.

She laughed and told me, "I now recognize how much I overrated my importance to all these people. The truth was that I had it backward. They were my foils because with them I could hide from myself. Stepping away from my own rat race, I finally saw what everyone else could see all along. I'd lost touch with my Spirit, and I was only fooling myself into thinking that I didn't need it."

### Tuning In

Your Spirit is the Divine fire in you, the spark of life, the creative catalyst for all things, and it must be respected and allowed to express itself. If not, it finds outlets elsewhere, often ones that are undesirable and can even feel destructive. The fire of your Spirit wants to clear away the things that block your authentic Self because they're stealing your life force. Sometimes your inner fire turns to rage when you try to overly control it or put it out, as it did with Barbara. Or your fire may be redirected in passive-aggressive ways, causing you to lash out at family and friends in order to relieve your internal conflict. If you suppress your inner fire long enough, it turns so far inward that it can even disturb your health. It can do any of these things to get your attention.

No matter how it expresses itself, your Spirit will not be muffled forever. Eventually, your inner fire will ignite and help you create an authentic life, filled with energy and awe; or it will "burn the house down," liberating you from the prison cell built up by your ego. You decide.

One way or another, all of us in time will be asked to surrender to the fire of our Spirit, to return to our original blueprint as Divine beings, because doing so will allow us to tap into our authentic personal power. The first commandment tells us not to have false gods. I believe this refers to the fears the mind becomes enslaved to that keep us ignoring the intuitive guidance in our hearts, making us dependent upon external things or our own misguided attempts to be in control at all times.

When we humble our controlling egos and take the leap and let go, our Spirit is liberated to create, evolve, and expand to unlimited horizons. Unless we take the leap, however, we cut ourselves off from our Divine power and burn out. Then we're left to rise from the ashes and find our way back to a genuine life once again. In the end, there is no other place to go.

### Asking the Questions

Close your eyes and calmly breathe in and out through your nose. Start with a sigh or two to help you relax. Massage your jaw and throat a little to release even more tension and fear held in that part of your body, your expression center. Feel the energetic tension that your racing mind creates in your body. Do you notice how it drains your energy, your life force, your kefi, right out of you?

Now relax the tension in your neck and throat as much as possible with a few gentle stretches and take in a deep, easy, belly-filling breath. Don't force your breath to enter your body by raising your shoulders and holding your head back. Rather, keep your shoulders comfortably relaxed and down, and allow your belly to pull the air in naturally without any tension at all. Exhale by releasing the sound "Ah," and then bring the corners of your lips up to your ears in a gentle smile.

Next, take out your journal and turn your attention inward. Contemplate each of the following questions and invite your Spirit, your most authentic Self, to respond to each one. Give yourself plenty of time to feel the genuine response coming from your heart, the source of your intuitive wisdom.

- What are you feeling most depressed, annoyed, irritated, restricted, frustrated, or angry about? Be specific.

- In what ways might you be feeling trapped? Or perhaps caught in a vicious cycle?

- In what ways might you be feeling burned out? Describe how you feel mentally and physically.

- What is your ego attached to most? Are there certain areas in your life that you feel you can't release control of?

- What are you most insecure about or afraid of? In what areas of your life do you feel that you really need support right now?

- Do you feel the fire of your Spirit within? Are you burning with passion and creativity, or smoldering with frustration?

- Can you sense the energy and spark that your Spirit ignites? Describe it.

- Where must you surrender control in order to reach for a more fulfilling expression of your inner fire?

- If you were to completely surrender to your intuition and follow its guidance, what would change first in your life?

- In what areas of your life do you most feel the need to trust others more?

After writing down your answers, set aside your journal and remain seated. Close your eyes and calmly breathe in and out through your nose. Start with a sigh or two to help you relax. Is your inner fire burning bright? Surrender control so that your Spirit can ignite your passion and creative spark.

With your next breath, let all of your tension go and simply *be* for a moment or two, even longer if possible. Enjoy sitting and breathing deeply, empty of all thought, free of any agenda, centered in the moment. Feel this vibration of being connected to Source. Notice how peaceful, content, and even energized you feel. This is the power of your Spirit, and it's available to you at all times. It is the real you. *Remember this.*

### Daily Ritual: Keep Your Fire Burning

Tend to the fire of your Spirit daily. Every morning, gently stretch, move, bend, or walk for at least five minutes shortly after awakening. Whether expressed in a few yoga postures, a trip to the gym, or a simple walk around the block, physical movement keeps your Spirit burning strong and channels its power toward your highest creative expression. Being stagnant or spending too much time "in your head" while sedentary causes the fire to die out.

It's vital to keep your inner fire fueled. Direct its power by sitting in quiet meditation for at least five minutes a day after your morning movement. In yoga, this balance is achieved through *savasana,* which means taking a few moments to quietly meditate and relax following the more active yoga *asanas,* or positions. Sit in your own version of savasana and listen to your intuition. Surrender your mind to your inner guidance, and let its fire be the force that moves you.

### The Ultimate Leap

The greatest leap we're ever asked to make is that of letting go of control, especially when we're facing our own death. Even then our Spirit is at hand, guiding us through the storm. Coming to know this is one of the greatest steps toward inner freedom and joyful living one can experience.

Bianca had gone through a terrible three-year period. Her beloved father was in a horrific accident at work that left him in a coma and paralyzed from the neck down. He never fully regained consciousness, and after two agonizing years in the hospital, he finally died. The impact of his death was devastating to the family, but especially to Bianca's younger brother, who fell into a deep depression. Feeling overwhelmed and demoralized, and unable to get past his father's passing, he took his own life, further shocking and crippling Bianca and her mother and sister.

Thankfully, her husband, who was her rock, kept her and their three young children going. Bianca ran a medical clinic for underprivileged women and couldn't afford to collapse into a state of emotional despair, for financial reasons as well as a personal obligation to the community she served.

Bianca was strongly tuned in to her intuition and knew in her mind, if only sometimes in her heart, that these horrendous losses might make sense one day. At the very least, she knew that eventually she might be able to accept what had happened and come to some sense of peace. This awareness kept her sane, yet at the same time she felt emotionally shut down and numb. Nevertheless, she had to remain strong for her clients, as well as for her mom and sister, who both seemed ready to collapse and give up. But most important, she had to appear cheerful for her children, who were still quite young and deserved a happy mother. She made sure to grieve out of sight and on the go.

Through early morning walks, late-night talks with her husband, and lots of daily prayer, Bianca managed to stay aloft. She took days off when she could, saw a massage therapist on occasion, went out to lunch with close friends, and practiced gratitude for everything in her life. She knew she had to be proactive and responsible for her own spiritual well-being, and that for some unknown reason, losing her loved ones was a lesson she had to undergo. She had to surrender to life as it unfolded, and she did her very best to do so.

It wasn't easy, as her emotions often clouded the scene. Her mother angered her with her constant negativity, acting so helpless and victimized, as if the loss was hers alone, while ignoring the fact that Bianca was suffering as well. Her sister was a little better. At least they could commiserate together when they needed to vent, both struggling with their mother and her self-absorbed grief, while also trying to console each other. It helped.

All in all, as sloppy and slow as it was, her efforts to surrender were working. She wasn't sure if she was surrendering to her Spirit or simply resigning herself to the circumstances life had dealt her, but she was doing her best. Eventually she had even recovered enough of her inner spark to suggest to her husband that they go to Disneyland for vacation, something the kids had begged them to do for years. In the spirit of getting on with life, it was time. Everyone was overjoyed.

Off they went on a wonderful family adventure, staying at one of the Disney hotels, enjoying the park to its fullest. Even Bianca admitted that it was a great, if not exhausting, vacation. The kids were entertained beyond their wildest imaginations, and their joy was infectious. It uplifted her.

After a week of fun and sun, they boarded their plane back home. They were on a smaller-sized aircraft and were seated near the back, all in one row. The flight was uneventful until they were close to landing. They suddenly flew into severely stormy weather with intense turbulence. They were on approach to land and experienced jolting wind shears just before touchdown, which nearly flipped over the airplane. The pilot aborted the landing. The lurch in her gut from this sudden drop was beyond anything Bianca had just paid to experience at Disneyland. This was truly frightening. Many passengers on the plane screamed in terror, and then everyone was silent.

The weather was so bad that it looked black outside. The plane was rocking violently when Bianca suddenly realized they were all going to die. At first she grabbed hold of her children's hands, although her son pushed her away. She started to recite the Hail Mary out loud, over and over again, almost as if in a trance, as the rest of the passengers remained silent in abject fear.

A second attempt was made to bring the plane in, and the same thing happened. The wind shears were so severe that the pilot again had to abort the landing at the last minute, and they rocketed through the storm, trying to regain altitude. Bianca couldn't stop praying, all the while thinking, *At least my family is together. When we die, no one will be left behind.*

Then something miraculous occurred. Bianca stopped fighting the experience they were in and completely surrendered to it instead. If they were going to die, she thought, that also meant that they were going to see God. She was suddenly overcome by a sense of profound peace and joy. It was unlike anything she had ever felt. In a wave of deep relaxation, she completely let go. Hugging her kids, even her son, who had somehow relaxed as well, they sat together serenely. In fact, she noticed that the more peaceful she was, the more her family followed her lead. It even seemed to spread in waves to other passengers. She could tell because many of the people near her were breathing regularly, almost in unison.

The storm outside was raging, but the one in her heart seemed to have lifted. She wondered if her father had felt this way before he died. She even wondered whether her brother had experienced this before he took his life. If so, she understood why he would go through with it. Never before had she felt such peace, knowing that she and her precious family would soon return to God, to Source.

The pilot approached the runway for the third time. This time, the plane slammed down hard on the ground and skidded, but they made it. After a moment of stunned silence, the passengers erupted into a roar of applause. The nightmare was over. They were alive and safe.

Yet Bianca was not the same woman. Somehow, during that harrowing experience, she had managed to completely surrender control. She let go of trying to make life go one way or another— instead she fully experienced what was. Her mind stopped trying to control everything, and her heart burst wide open. It didn't matter if she died that day. She'd discovered what lies beyond this realm, beyond her control . . . and it was beautiful beyond belief.

Something else also happened. She realized at the same time that there was no reason to resist the earthly realm either. In other words, life wasn't meant to be controlled, managed, resisted, judged, or feared. It was just meant to be lived, and that was something she had been afraid of. But now she knew there was no right or wrong way—she was just supposed to fully experience everything. Right after the plane miraculously landed, Bianca burst out laughing, overcome with joy. She was so thankful they made it, because she knew she had a lot of living to make up for. Since the Universe had decided to give her more time, she didn't want to waste another moment feeling bad.

To Bianca, life had never looked or felt so good. Her children were miracles before her eyes. Her husband was beautiful. The blue sky, just peeking through the now lifting heavy clouds was spectacular. Colors seemed brighter, the air was crisp, and the sounds around her were music to her ears. She wasn't sure where she had been all these years, but she was present now! And she was no longer afraid. What a relief. What a gift to have been on that plane. She laughed all the way home, and hasn't stopped since.

### Tuning In

The ultimate leap is to stop living in the past or future, stop yearning for the approval of others, and stop trying to control the situation, or life itself. Simply experience life as it comes instead. This is a profound transformational shift because the ego doesn't know how to do this, and maybe never will. The highest form of surrender is when you free yourself from your ego's perceptions and experience life from the full vantage point of your Spirit. Because you are only temporarily in a physical form, death to this form is inevitable. The ego game is to pretend that it won't happen, but this takes you away from fully living and enjoying life.

Accepting death is the ultimate leap of faith and the highest form of transformation to Spirit. We have no choice. But when we accept death to the best of our ability, we are given the most powerful gift of life—the freedom to fully live as our authentic selves.

### Asking the Questions

Close your eyes and calmly breathe in and out through your nose. Start with a sigh or two to help you relax. Massage your jaw and throat a little to release even more tension and fear held in that part of your body, your expression center. Feel the energetic tension that your racing mind creates in your body. Do you notice how it drains your energy, your life force, your kefi, right out of you?

Now relax the tension in your neck and throat as much as possible with a few gentle stretches and take in a deep, easy, belly-filling breath. Don't force your breath to enter your body by raising your shoulders and holding your head back. Rather, keep your shoulders comfortably relaxed and down, and allow your belly to pull the air in naturally without any tension at all. Exhale by releasing the sound "Ah," and then bring the corners of your lips up to your ears in a gentle smile.

Next, take out your journal and turn your attention inward. Contemplate each of the following questions, and invite your Spirit, your most authentic Self, to respond to each one. Give yourself plenty of time to feel the genuine response coming from your heart, the source of your power.

- Have you experienced the death of a loved one? Describe what happened.

- How do you presently feel about death and dying? Do you ever think about it? Do you ignore it, fear it, or perhaps accept it?

- What ideas do you hold about life after death?

- What connection, if any, have you ever had to the afterlife? For example, have you ever dreamed of someone who died? Have you ever had an out-of-body or near-death experience? Has someone close to you ever had this kind of experience?

- If you knew you were dying, what would you do differently? Can you start doing this now? Why or why not?

After writing down your answers, set aside your journal and remain seated. Close your eyes and calmly breathe in and out through your nose. Start with a sigh or two to help you relax. Can you let go of any fears you have about death? Tune in to your intuition, the power of your Spirit, and to the best of your ability release your desire to control life. Feel the profound serenity that comes with relaxing.

With your next breath, let all of your tension go and simply *be* for a moment or two, even longer if possible. Enjoy sitting and breathing deeply, empty of all thought, free of any agenda, centered in the moment. Feel this vibration of being connected to God. Notice how peaceful, content, and even energized you feel. This is the power of your Spirit, and it's available to you at all times. It is the real you. *Remember this.*

### Daily Ritual: Live Your Love

Rarely does someone truly know when the hour of death will arrive. Thus, rather than focusing on when that will happen, this practice asks you to fully live instead. Today—right now—make a list of all the things you want to do or experience before you leave this life. Create your "bucket list," so to speak.

Put this list in a prominent place, one where you can't miss it, and then do one thing toward fulfilling it every day, without exception. Live as if you no longer have the time to put off your dreams or answer to someone else's demands, rather than your own authentic desires. You really don't have the time!

Ignore all the reasons your ego comes up with to make you put this off or believe that other things are more important. Your ego is lying to you once again. There is no reason why you shouldn't live as you wish, starting right now. To do so is the greatest leap of faith . . . and with it comes the gift of life.

☀

Congratulations on making it this far! Relax and take a deep cleansing breath. Have you made time to listen to your intuition every day? Has it helped you discover your authentic Self and connect with your Spirit? Be sure to note how you're feeling in your journal, and keep track of the changes you're experiencing (in yourself and others).

The last step of transformation is the most exciting of all. Are you ready to *enter the flow?*

# Chapter Six

# STEP FOUR:
# ENTERING THE FLOW

When you enter the flow, your ego steps aside and allows your Spirit to completely take over. You receive uninterrupted guidance, direction, solutions, gifts, and even positive surprises from the Universe every day. You place complete trust in the Universe to take care of you in every circumstance and situation you encounter. You can expect assistance with every problem or challenge that arises, and you will receive it.

When you are in the flow, you move through each day in a state of optimism, gratitude, receptivity, and flexibility—ready and willing at any moment to change plans, move in a different direction, and follow your intuition without hesitation or fear. You feel protected because you know you have Divine helpers, both on this plane and in Spirit, who accompany you every step of the way. You expect the best and miraculously attract it, over and over again. Interestingly, it might not be quite what you envisioned, but it will always be the best of what is possible, which is more often than not a much better version than you could have ever imagined.

You feel fully connected to the web of life and move in guided, synchronistic harmony with all, without questioning how things might work out. You simply trust they will. There is no space between you and life, so you experience no interruption or interference from your controlling intellect. Life falls into beautiful cooperation with you, and you with it, in a harmonious dance. One of my clients described flowing with her intuition as "living a charmed life—one that keeps getting better and better." Another referred to it as the "how good can you stand it" experience of life. A third said that it's "God in the driver's seat with you buckled in for the ride of a lifetime with the best chauffeur there is."

Whatever you call it, when in *flow* you experience ease, grace, peace, healing, and connection. Divine forces behind the scenes connect all the dots of your life, so you can simply enjoy the experience as it unfolds. The best part is the freedom from stress and worry that it offers. You find yourself feeling genuinely carefree and confident, like a well-loved and cared-for child, surrendered in trust.

Mihaly Csikszentmihalyi, in his book *Flow,* refers to this as the optimal human experience. He affirms that people in flow create an inner state of being that brings them peace and fulfillment that's separate from their external environment. In other words, it's an experience that is completely free of the ego's control or fearful response to the outside world. Flow occurs when you tune in to your intuition, trust what you feel in your heart, live in the present moment, and move in sync with life—rather than struggle against it. When in flow, you and Spirit are one.

Everyone has experienced episodes of flow from time to time—some for a few minutes, some for hours, and some longer. Yet when you become a truly transformed human—living as a Divine being as opposed to a divided and struggling ego-centered being—flow becomes more of a constant. You may have forgetful moments and slip back into a temporary mental state of worry, resistance, and fear; but once you experience flow, these episodes become shorter and are less frequent. Fear and worry cease to torment you as they once may have. Your intuition, your Spirit, leads your life, while your ego-mind, now the faithful servant of the Spirit, steps aside. Once you've experienced this, you can trust that you will find it again.

Flow is often perceived as luck by the spiritually unaware, but there's really nothing lucky or coincidental about it. Flow is faith in action: the synthesis of your true authentic nature merging with your faith in God, the Universe, and life. It is the natural consequence of living as a Divine spiritual being, expressing your most authentic Self, and following your intuition. When in flow, you're learning to be a Divine co-creator, making life an exhilarating and joyous adventure.

Not only is flow a personally beautiful and expanded experience, but your positive energy also has an undisputable, immediately infectious effect on others. The minute you're around someone who is in flow, your own vibration quickly elevates, and you start to resonate in greater harmony with life. You feel positive, confident, and creative. Your heart opens, and your compassion expands to higher and more perceptive levels.

In other words, you feel inspired, which means *taking the Spirit in.* When your Spirit is "home," fully present in you—moving through your limbs, expressing itself through your mind, living though your heart—everyone around you feels this energy and is profoundly affected.

### The Surprise Visit

I was recently reminded of the power of Spirit in flow in the most unexpected way. My family and several of our neighbors decided to have a big barbecue together. We seized upon the idea with great enthusiasm, and it wasn't long before it had extended well beyond the neighborhood.

When our closest neighbors Craig and Sarah showed up, they brought along Sarah's brother, his wife, and their three kids, including a gawky, painfully shy 14-year-old boy. He sat quietly on the couch and kept to himself the entire time, barely saying a word to anyone. More than once I noticed him sitting alone and asked if he was having fun, and he responded with a faint smile and an unconvincing "yes." Obviously, he preferred that I leave him alone rather than make a lame effort at conversation, so I smiled back and left him by himself.

Hours later, the party got livelier, but this young man's demeanor remained the same. He wasn't down—he was just extremely flat, as if no one was home. However, that changed after everyone was finished eating. His mother suddenly announced to all of us that it was time to gather around the piano and listen to her son's latest musical creation. As we walked toward the piano, the boy's dad turned to me and explained that his son had only taken one lesson, so I thoroughly expected this already very shy teen to suffer even more as he was made to perform. Was I ever wrong!

The minute that quiet young man placed his hands on the piano keys, he transformed. He came *alive*. From out of nowhere, his energy shifted, and I could feel his Spirit take over. His fingers flew like lightning across the keyboard, and he unfurled a musical masterpiece that took everyone's breath away. His playing was stunning. Watching him was dizzying; his music was so moving, so heartfelt, that it was as if he'd pulled it right out of heaven. This performance was clearly not streaming from his intellect. After all, he'd only taken one lesson his entire life! No, without question, it was his Spirit playing the piano, and it was so powerful and gorgeous that it humbled us all.

When he finished, everyone—kids and adults—fell silent for a moment and then burst into enormous applause. His Spirit shone brilliantly through his music, and it flowed with a force of its own. When it was over, people just shook their heads in amazement. There were no words to express the experience.

The most impressive thing about this spontaneous spirited visitation, at least for me, was that it didn't end that night. I still felt its power the next day and clear into the evening. Several times I found myself sharing the experience of him playing with people I ran into. It was too potent to keep it to myself. Later the following night, I wasn't surprised when my friend Debra, who had also been at the barbecue, brought it up while we were chatting. She, too, was still feeling the effects of his spirited concert. We laughingly shook our heads in awe, remarking about the tangible power he'd expressed. A moment later, in came my daughter, and without knowing what we were talking about, she also brought up the young piano player's performance and how much it was on her mind. In the end, we all agreed that we'd witnessed something special that made us want to express our own Spirit as authentically and powerfully as he had.

This was a beautiful example of the power of one person's Spirit to uplift, inspire, excite, and activate the vibration and creativity in all people. This boy's Spirit in flow made our Spirits want to flow with his. That is how powerful your Spirit is! We may all express our Divine selves differently, but it is the same Holy Spirit coming through. For the young boy, it was expressed though the piano's keys. For someone else, it might be expressed through the keys of a computer. It may come through baking a pie, planting a garden, or even sweeping the porch. It doesn't matter what we're doing really—what does matter is that when the Spirit is doing the "doing" of our life, it becomes magical.

We all have things we must tend to every day. If our ego is solely in charge, we might undertake them in a begrudging, long-suffering, resentful, or unloving way. The work gets done, but the effort drains us and those around us. But if we allow our Spirit to express through us and let it be the "doer," whether in work or play, the act itself instantly becomes a powerful expression. It is "love made visible," as the famous Lebanese-American novelist and poet Kahlil Gibran wrote in his beautiful book *The Prophet*.

If each of us would flow with the natural expression of our Spirit in all that we do, we would serve to awaken it in others, and soon the entire planet would gracefully flow together. I believe that this is the Divine plan. We just have to get on with it! That is what the grand transformation from ego to Spirit is all about.

## Tuning In

Entering the flow of your Spirit isn't as challenging or far-out as it may seem—despite what your ego may be telling you. Everyone has experienced flowing with Spirit in one way or another. Think of the times you've become so engaged and immersed in doing something you love that you've lost all track of time and space. You were so content, so happily involved in the experience, that you felt as if you could carry on forever.

When in flow, we are love in motion. Time, space, and separation from life cease to exist. We merge with our experiences and become one. Whether it's cooking a meal, doing the laundry, or washing the car, all of us have flowed with things that we've had to do and express at one point or another—probably more often than we realize. We just need to learn to be in the flow a lot more.

The way to flow is to become committed to doing things we love every day. This doesn't mean to suggest that we must do them all day to be successful, or exclusively. A little bit of time that is free of worry, or resistance to life, and involved in something that provides either a break from thinking (such as folding laundry) or involves thinking in a new, creative, engaging way, such as working on a favorite hobby that requires a bit of skill is all that's needed to enter the flow. This is because flow is the act of being free of thinking, thus entering either a quiet inner space when we simply are *being* or fearlessly expressing our true Self. Flow feels like being in a state of grace.

## Asking the Questions

Close your eyes and calmly breathe in and out through your nose. Start with a sigh or two to help you relax. Massage your jaw and throat a little to release even more tension and fear held in that part of your body, your expression center. Feel the energetic tension that your racing mind creates in your body. Do you notice how it drains your energy, your life force, your kefi, right out of you?

Now relax the tension in your neck and throat as much as possible with a few gentle stretches and take in a deep, easy, belly-filling breath. Don't force your breath to enter your body by raising your shoulders and holding your head back. Rather, keep your shoulders comfortably relaxed and down, and allow your belly to pull the air in naturally without any tension at all. Exhale by releasing the sound "Ah," and then bring the corners of your lips up to your ears in a gentle smile.

Next, take out your journal and turn your attention inward. Contemplate each of the following questions and tune in to your Spirit, your most authentic Self, to respond to each one. Give yourself plenty of time to feel the genuine response coming from your heart, the source of your true power.

- What do you love doing? Do you love to sing, dance, or play an instrument? Do you love going to work every day or playing with your kids? Do you love to golf, exercise, do yard work, or go jogging with your dog? Be specific. How do you feel when you're doing what you love?

- What can you do so well that it's a pure joy to do it?

- When you're deeply engaged, can you sense that your Spirit is taking over? How would you describe flowing with your Spirit to someone?

- Recall a moment when you were so fully engaged in something that you lost all track of time. What were you doing?

- If you could do anything you wanted to, what would you do? This doesn't have to be work related—it can be anything at all.

- When was the last time you experienced someone else in flow? What was he or she doing? How did it affect you?

- When was the last time you felt clearly *out* of flow? What were you doing? What were you thinking? What were you resisting at the time?

- Where do you feel most in flow in your life? Where do you feel least in flow?

After writing down your answers, set aside your journal and remain seated. Close your eyes and calmly breathe in and out through your nose. Start with a sigh or two to help you relax. Call to mind something you love to do and tune in to the way your body feels. When you're aligned with your genuine Self, you're flowing with your Spirit.

With your next breath, let all of your tension go and simply *be* for a moment or two, even longer if possible. Enjoy sitting and breathing deeply, empty of all thought, free of any agenda, centered in the moment. Feel this vibration of being connected to Source. Notice how peaceful, content, and even energized you feel. This is the power of your Spirit, and it's available to you at all times. It is the real you. *Remember this.*

### Daily Ritual: Go with the Flow

Going with the flow means accepting life exactly as it is. If you're stuck in traffic, for example, flow with the slower pace rather than honking your horn and cursing at the "idiots" on the road. If you're in a hurry at the grocery store and the checkout line is at a standstill, take a few breaths, smile, and laugh at the tabloid headlines rather than complaining or crowding the people ahead of you to get things moving. If you're working on a project and run into every possible obstacle, step back, take a short break, and adjust your approach to allow some space to enter and relieve the logjam.

In other words, make it a habit to *relax*. Let go. Take a breath and look around. Enjoy the view. Accept life as it unfolds, rather than try to force it in a particular way. Don't complain just for the sake of it, or struggle as a matter of habit. Don't fight to be first. Be patient, and turn to your intuition for guidance instead. Be aware, listen, and move in accordance with its vibration. Meet what comes your way with grace. Flowing with your Spirit is when you acknowledge the beauty, wisdom, and purpose of what is and cooperate with life as opposed to fighting against it.

You may experience setbacks, but everyone does at times. It's not uncommon to lose your patience (or your temper) and feel tempted to give someone a piece of your mind or want to tell someone else how he or she "should" be living. But reactions and patterned responses like these simply take you out of the flow. They're also upsetting to you and others. Resistance accomplishes nothing of value. Even if you manage to force someone into doing things your way, the negative energy that goes along with your "win" isn't worth the fight. You'll experience the backlash of such bullying later on—count on it. You'll get much further in life by feeling and following the flow than you will by bumping up against it.

This doesn't mean that you should be passive or meek. You just need to be aware of the energy around you and use it instead of fighting it. Take, for example, those who practice martial arts. They follow the flow and use the energy coming toward them to diffuse an attack rather than resist it. The force of the attacker is absorbed and transformed. The end result is that the martial artist remains safe, protected, and above all, peaceful, grounded, and unafraid.

When you do meet a setback, catch yourself and make adjustments as quickly as possible. Ask yourself if you have strayed from your inner truth or if this obstacle simply means it's time to accept present conditions as they unfold. Use your breath to reenter the flow. Remember to always breathe, tune in, accept, allow, enjoy, and flow.

### The Ebb

The greatest challenge to staying in flow comes when you encounter "the ebb," which is any change, expected or unexpected, that leaves you feeling threatened and insecure because you aren't sure what's coming next. You may wonder or worry if you can handle it, if the change will be harmful or difficult, or even if you'll be safe.

I experienced an intense and unexpected ebb many years ago when the job I held at the time, as an international flight attendant, suddenly came to an end. The union I belonged to declared a strike, and we all walked out. Being young and unhappy with certain aspects of my job, I eagerly joined my co-workers on the picket line, but fully expected to return to work after a few days of company-versus-union arguments. I figured I'd be back to flying to Paris and London in no time at all.

Instead, all of the striking flight attendants were immediately replaced with new hires, and the door to our jobs closed behind us with a slam. I was so shocked, surprised, and insulted that I just couldn't believe it. That wasn't at all what I had expected to occur. "How could the company do this?!" I shouted to my friends and anyone else who would listen. "I didn't deserve this! The company was evil to do this to all these good people—especially me," I proclaimed with righteous indignation. "Now what will I do to survive?"

But my indignant, furious, insulted, wounded, and most of all, frightened outpouring didn't make a difference. Much as I didn't want them to, my circumstances had indeed changed. My mind was racing: *What about my free airline passes? How will I pay my rent or buy groceries? What about my co-workers who live elsewhere? How will we be able to see each other again? How will I ever get back to Denver to visit my parents? Or go on adventures?* Such big and little unknowns frightened me and left me feeling overwhelmed by a force far greater than I was.

For weeks, I panicked and fretted. Then I realized, to my surprise, that once I was away from the job, I was actually glad to be free of it. I admitted to myself that I'd never loved it, and truthfully, I'd always felt a bit like an imposter wearing the uniform. I loved the benefits—traveling to new places, meeting new people—but I wasn't using my gifts the way I had wanted to, and that had always bothered me. While I was on strike, I was suddenly free to pursue what I loved and so, void of interference, I turned my full and undivided attention to my intuitive work for the first time in my life.

I began to book intuitive readings with clients on a regular basis, many of whom were my flight-attendant friends, and helped them discover ways to work through the job crisis. I also started teaching monthly workshops in my studio apartment. It was the most challenging, exciting, and fulfilling thing I'd ever done in my life. I didn't want to stop! I was even able to sign up for dance and yoga classes on a regular basis (another love), which was not possible when I worked as a flight attendant because my schedule had been much too irregular. I never would have done any of this if the strike hadn't occurred. Although I hadn't really loved my job, I'd liked it well enough that I never considered quitting. Thankfully, it quit me.

My worst nightmare surprisingly became my greatest gift. While kicking and screaming though the ebb, I took the leap and trusted my intuition completely, followed my heart, and committed fully to my true life's purpose and vocation of spiritual and intuitive guidance work, which I still do and love to this day. Had that ebb not occurred, I might still be a flight attendant and would have missed the joy and satisfaction of living my dream for all these years. And that is a scary thought.

In retrospect, I can see clearly just how ready for change my Spirit was. Behind the fear of change rose the challenge to push past my limiting circumstances, be creative, and trust my intuition to guide me to the next step, which is exactly what I did.

Although my response to the ebb was sloppy and emotional at first—and my ego milked the drama for all it could—several years later, when I was offered the chance to return to the airline, I couldn't fathom going back. I was way too happy where I was.

I still am! Thank goodness for the ebb, because it was necessary for me to get into a higher flow. That is what the ebb in life is all about.

### Tuning In

Ebbs occur all the time. They are natural because change is inevitable—nothing remains the same indefinitely. Life moves in cycles, and when you encounter an ebb, it just means that it's time for that cycle to change. Ebbs occur on a global scale as well as on a personal one. A global ebb may come about as a dramatic shift in the current state of the economy or government; or it might appear as an extreme climate or environmental change, such as an earthquake, volcanic eruption, hurricane, or tsunami. These natural ebbs have been around since the beginning of time and will continue till the end of time.

Ebbs arise as our personal life cycles shift. We enter an ebb, for example, when we go from being at home all day to our first day of school, which means leaving the familiarity and safety of our caregivers and entering the unknown. For some children, this feels like a catastrophe, but in the end, these same kids learn to adjust, grow, and eventually come to greatly enjoy this new experience. We usually kick and scream when the ebbs of life arrive, but if we choose to respond to them as creative conscious Spirits, these changes activate great evolutionary leaps, liberating us from unnecessary and illusory dependencies that we no longer need.

Ebbs don't necessarily feel good, but they are important disruptions because they instigate growth that we wouldn't ordinarily do on our own. We're invited to tune in to where we are, become aware of patterns that hold us back, and enter a new cycle that pushes us ahead. Ebbs require us to let go of ego complacencies and engage our intuition so that we can be fluid, flexible, creative, and solution oriented. The climactic ebb in the human experience is transitioning into death, leading to the flow of rebirth in our Spirit form.

As conscious beings entering the great transformation from *Homo sapiens* to *Homo spiritus,* we must expect, even embrace, the ebb and be willing to move in a new and often unexplored direction without hesitation. This can feel extremely destabilizing and threatening to the ego (which is the Divine plan), causing us to feel anxious, stressed, victimized, overwhelmed, and powerless. That's why it's vital to expect periods of ebb in the flow of life, and recognize that this is a signal from our Spirit that it's once again time to grow.

Even though ebbs are unwelcome to the ego, which wants to be in control and doesn't like change, they remind us that the ego never really was in control. The ebbs of life invite us to flow no matter what, and especially to flow in a way that's compatible with change. Ebbs activate our intuition to override the ego and creatively respond to life by reaching inside and freeing up new insights and solutions. The ebbs of life can be viewed as psychic calisthenics for the Spirit, which take away our mental crutches and make us stronger, freer, and more powerful.

Entering a cycle of growth can feel dramatic, scary, and threatening—as if your very self is under attack—but if you remember to surrender to your intuition and go with the flow, the ebb will guide you to better and better versions of yourself. When the ebb appears in the flow, it simply means that a greater version of you is ready to make its appearance.

The ebb of life reveals which attachments no longer serve your soul purpose in the best way and what keeps you from being of highest service to the planet. It is actually a signal that you're graduating from a certain *step* of awareness or experience and are now ready to move to the next level. Therefore, always expect the ebb to be part of the flow as long as you are in human form, because growth into Divine consciousness is the only purpose for being here.

To be in the flow means to fully trust your intuition and know that your Spirit can create a positive outcome out of any circumstance that comes its way, no matter what. To flow is to believe that the Universe is always conspiring for your success as a spiritual being, that all that unfolds is part of your grand soul plan, inviting you to move closer to your more authentic self.

### Asking the Questions

Close your eyes and calmly breathe in and out through your nose. Start with a sigh or two to help you relax. Massage your jaw and throat a little to release even more tension and fear held in that part of your body, your expression center. Feel the energetic tension that your racing mind creates in your body. Do you notice how it drains your energy, your life force, your kefi, right out of you?

Now relax the tension in your neck and throat as much as possible with a few gentle stretches and take in a deep, easy, belly-filling breath. Don't force your breath to enter your body by raising your shoulders and holding your head back. Rather, keep your shoulders comfortably relaxed and down, and allow your belly to pull the air in naturally without any tension at all. Exhale by releasing the sound "Ah," and then bring the corners of your lips up to your ears in a gentle smile.

Next, take out your journal and turn your attention inward. Contemplate each of the following questions and tune in to your Spirit, your most authentic Self, to respond to each one. Give yourself plenty of time to feel the genuine response coming from your heart, the source of your power.

- What cycle are you in now: ebb or flow?

- What aspect of your life is in ebb? How do you know?

- If you are in an ebb cycle, what does your Spirit want to unleash? Tune in and ask.

- What unexpected challenges are inviting you to grow? Be specific.

- Are you clinging to old beliefs or aspects of yourself? In what ways? How does holding on, rather than letting go and growing, make you feel? Are you forgetting that you are a Divine being and instead feeling more like a victim?

- If you are in the flow, when was the last time you were in an ebb cycle? What gifts and talents have the ebb of life revealed that you weren't aware of beforehand?

After writing down your answers, set aside your journal and remain seated. Close your eyes and calmly breathe in and out through your nose. Start with a sigh or two to help you relax. Think about cycles of ebb during your life. Knowing the end re-sults, can you see the ways in which these personal shifts brought you in deeper alignment with your Spirit?

With your next breath, let all of your tension go and simply *be* for a moment or two, even longer if possible. Enjoy sitting and breathing deeply, empty of all thought, free of any agenda, cen-tered in the moment. Feel this vibration of being connected to Source. Notice how peaceful, content, and even energized you feel. This is the power of your Spirit, and it's available to you at all times. It is the real you. *Remember this.*

### Daily Ritual: Embrace the Ebb

Notice how life flows in cycles. Are you in the flow or the ebb? If you're flowing with your Spirit, carry on; and if you're in an ebb cycle, accept it. Don't fight against change. Just tune in, be aware, and acknowledge that all things are in Divine order at all times.

Remember that no one can go through life without encoun-tering ebbs, but you will eventually return to flow. The more con-sciously you accept this, the quicker the ebb turns back to flow and the longer the period of uninterrupted flow will continue. When in ebb, recognize that it has great value. Study what the ebb is asking you to release, and move on. It's a signal that it's time to grow—you're ready to advance to the next soul step. Whether in ebb or flow, communicate your true values and priorities, state your goals, and allow your intuition to lead you.

## The Miracle

Being in flow isn't a stagnant condition or a one-way street. Even the direction of flow can change at times, and does. When it does change, it's up to us to quiet our reactions and go inward, and listen to our intuition so that we can creatively respond to the change of course.

Emily, a freelance writer, consciously practiced living in flow. On the days that all went according to plan, it was easy. She felt confident and relaxed, even a bit smug that she was "in the know" about higher living. On the days that life surprised her, however, she felt challenged, annoyed, and afraid. But she was prepared. She knew to breathe, accept, allow, and trust that what was unfolding was in accordance with the Divine plan and not her own. On those days, in spite of her impulse to resist, she surrendered her ego to the reality at hand and accepted life as it was.

It wasn't as simple as it sounded, though. When life was heading into uncharted territory, Emily felt the same way she did when she was first learning to drive: hesitant and self-conscious. Nothing came automatically. She had to stop and think about her responses in order to be certain she was choosing those that aligned with her Spirit. Only then would she act. The hesitation created enormous tension in her body, followed by relief when she felt she'd made the correct choice. She got through each day, but her rhythm felt disjointed and stiff. It didn't feel natural to be so consciously deliberate, at least not yet.

But still she progressed, her intuition slowly coming more naturally as her commitment to Divine living increased. Perhaps as a way to reassure herself that going with the flow was the best way to live, she often enthusiastically shared this philosophy with her friends and loved ones. She was so persuasive and dynamic that people even began to seek her out when they felt insecure and threatened. Her "trust your intuition and go with the flow" speech calmed them. She spoke with such conviction that they trusted her and allowed themselves to surrender their fears and give it a try.

Emily was making adequate progress and even enjoying a degree of calm when she met with a series of unexpected financial disruptions that put her into a truly vulnerable, even potentially disastrous, position. First, her two primary magazines changed editors within a matter of weeks of each other, and both canceled her monthly columns without notice. Her primary sources of income vanished overnight, leaving her without enough money to cover the significant rent for her San Francisco apartment. Shortly after that, the IRS sent her a letter stating that she'd misfiled her taxes and owed $47,000, which was due within a few weeks of receiving the notice. She was horrified. Over the years, she'd been living paycheck to paycheck and had virtually no savings. Furthermore, she was a single woman in her 60s and had no children, family, or friends from whom she would feel comfortable borrowing such a large sum of money. She simply didn't have it and had absolutely no way to get it. So she was, in her words, "completely screwed."

For Emily, it was one thing to trust her intuition and go with the flow when it came to getting along with others, delivering articles on time, and generally making ends meet by controlling her shopping and other unnecessary indulgences. But it was quite another when she was suddenly faced with unemployment, bankruptcy, possible eviction, and a tax conviction by the IRS. All of a sudden "going with the flow" seemed naive and ridiculous, an irresponsible Pollyanna perspective that ignored the demands of real life.

And yet, what else could she do? Constantly worry? That would hardly solve her problem. Panic? She was already doing that, and it in no way relieved her of her dire straits. Collapse? Even if she did, no one would be there to pick her up and carry her forward. Run away? There was nowhere to go. Besides, even running would cost money, which she didn't have. None of these ego-motivated, victim-based responses provided any more relief than her "go with the flow" approach offered. This was beyond ebb. This was more than a dip in the climb. This was a complete collapse of her system, and she needed rescue in the form of a solution—and she needed it fast.

Her only option was to accept all that she had preached over the years and turn the entire problem over to the Universe and trust that it would help her solve it. In doing so, she first had to face her deepest fears and insecurities, the ones she thought she had long ago dispelled.

"Why would the Universe help you? After all, you created the problem!" her ego hissed. "If you had been more responsible over the years, this never would have happened. You should have saved. You should have checked on your accountant. You were wasteful and extravagant and foolishly spent too much money. In fact, given your arrogant and irresponsible behavior, you deserve to go to jail. Shame on you!"

Yes, shame. That is exactly the way Emily felt: completely and utterly ashamed. It was such a deep and old energy that she felt as if she had carried it forever. In fact, she was now sure she was born with it. Feeling it envelop her, she realized that it was this exact energy she had been running from her entire life. She thought she had outwitted it with her spiritual practice, only to find herself suddenly trapped. Her shame quickly closed in on her, laughing as if to say, "So you thought you escaped me, did you? You can never escape!"

Emily felt it shroud her entire being, like a dark, life-sucking cloud of death. And yet, she didn't die. She was absolutely miserable, but she wasn't dead. Confronting her deepest, most negative beliefs about herself, in the face of her greatest external fear of being completely out of control and vulnerable, Emily did something she had never done before. She started to laugh. At first, it was a nervous reflex. But soon enough it turned into genuine heartfelt laughter. It was the laughter of a profound realization. She *was* out of control. She hadn't a clue as to how to solve her dilemma. And it didn't kill her. She could relax and quit running. The more she laughed, the better she felt.

She suddenly understood that the only solution was to turn to God to solve the problem and guide her out of it. She realized her spiritual training period was over. She was no longer in the student's seat when it came to going with the flow of the Universe. She had to graduate, give up her reservations, and completely trust in Divine direction. There was no other way.

It was a leap of faith, and she took it. For the first time, she placed her full confidence and entire well-being in the hands of God and in her intuition. She got down on her knees and prayed for a solution. She didn't lament the problem, as she felt it would be useless to do so. If the Universe was to help, surely it understood the problem better than she did, so there was no need to go over it, further upsetting herself. No, she would not indulge.

Emily prayed for guidance. But as she did, she recognized, perhaps for the first time in her spiritual transformation, a deeper meaning of going with the flow. She wasn't simply to go with just any flow. She needed to align her personal creative intention with the highest flow of Divine creative intention and flow with that. She couldn't just pray to be rescued, as that would reduce her to a passive victim. She needed to pray for inspiration on how to solve the problem herself, to the best of her ability as a Divine being.

She asked to be shown the best way to turn her present situation into a creative example of Divine inspiration and flow. She prayed with her entire heart and soul to be relieved of all blockages, low self-esteem, and shame (known or unconscious). She prayed that her fears would be alleviated so that she could move forward in confidence. She prayed to be free of any disruption of peace in her life. She prayed until she could find no more words to pray. She prayed until her heart was calm and quiet. And then she stopped. There was nothing more to be done.

At that point, all Emily could do was be patient and wait. She was moved to go back to the work of her daily tasks because she needed to do *something*. So she cleaned her apartment, finished working on a few last articles that were due, and walked her dog. And when night came, she went to sleep. Small as they were, those actions felt comforting and right.

She continued her routine for the next several days, praying all the while to keep her stress at bay. On the third night, she awoke with a start. As soon as she opened her eyes, the idea and title for a book resounded in her mind. And it was a terrific title and a subject she could confidently write about. The minute she stated the title out loud, a wave of relief instantly swept over her. This was it. This was the solution. She immediately wrote it down and lay there in astonishment. She had never, ever considered writing a book, let alone one so clever. As she sat in awe, more ideas on the subject poured into her mind like a rushing river. She found a notebook and started jotting them down, grabbing on to them before they disappeared into the night.

The next morning she called her agent and ran the book idea past her. Not sure how her agent would respond, Emily was greatly surprised and relieved to get just as much enthusiasm from her agent as she herself had felt when the idea first came to her. Her agent suggested that she put pen to paper right away, and said she would start attempting to sell the idea.

So Emily wrote as her agent shopped the title to various publishers. Four weeks later, Emily had her first-ever book contract, along with an impressive advance of $125,000. After paying her agent, she would have enough left over to pay all back taxes, her credit-card debt, and rent for a few months. It was nothing short of a miracle.

But more than the miracle of solving her financial problems of the moment, she experienced the miracle of fully trusting in the Universe and her intuition to show her how to live as a Divine being rather than a victim. With this new experience as her foundation, she would never again fall back under the illusion that she must live in fear of things she cannot control, or of change itself. She was free and in the creative flow of a higher, Divine energy. That's what being a transformed, Divine being means: to live as a full creative partner with the Universe, setting an intention and then being open to the inspiration and guidance for that intention to be realized.

### Tuning In

Going with the flow of the Universe doesn't mean passively surrendering personal creativity and responsibility for the way your life unfolds. Rather, it means living with dynamic creative intention—aligning your personal creativity with the Divine plan so that the fulfillment of your intentions, needs, and desires is divinely supported, guided, and directed.

Simply put, tell the Universe what you want, but don't tell the Universe how you want it delivered. Leave yourself open to receiving inspiration and intuitive guidance on how best to create your intended desires at all times. Wait in confidence until the flow directs you. It will arrive in the form of intuition. Then follow the intuitive guidance you receive without hesitation or question. That's what it means to go with the flow at the highest level.

### Asking the Questions

Close your eyes and calmly breathe in and out through your nose. Start with a sigh or two to help you relax. Massage your jaw and throat a little to release even more tension and fear held in that part of your body, your expression center. Feel the energetic tension that your racing mind creates in your body. Do you notice how it drains your energy, your life force, your kefi, right out of you?

Now relax the tension in your neck and throat as much as possible with a few gentle stretches and take in a deep, easy, belly-filling breath. Don't force your breath to enter your body by raising your shoulders and holding your head back. Rather, keep your shoulders comfortably relaxed and down, and allow your belly to pull the air in naturally without any tension at all. Exhale by releasing the sound "Ah," and then bring the corners of your lips up to your ears in a gentle smile.

Next, take out your journal and turn your attention inward. Contemplate each of the following questions and invite your Spirit, your most authentic Self, to respond to each one. Give yourself plenty of time to feel the genuine response coming from your heart, your intuition, the source of your power.

- Have you ever needed to fully trust in the Universe for inspiration or direction? In what way? Describe the situation in detail.

- Are you a student or a seasoned pro when it comes to going with the flow?

- Do you easily tune in to your intuition? How so? Do you receive intuition through your gut feelings or dreams, or perhaps as an overall sense of knowing?

- Do you fully trust your intuition? In what areas do you trust it the most? When are you hesitant to trust it? Explain your reasoning.

- Are you in the habit of setting intentions and goals? Do you make commitments with confidence, or do you tend to avoid them?

- In what area of your life do you most want to receive guidance and direction right now?

- What are your heart's most important creative desires?

- Do you pray? Why or why not?

- Can you laugh at your fears? How does that make you feel?

- How has your intuition helped you lately?

- In what ways have you already been inspired and guided by the Universe?

After writing down your answers, set aside your journal and remain seated. Close your eyes and calmly breathe in and out through your nose. Start with a sigh or two to help you relax. Tune in to your higher self and wait for guidance. Trust your intuition, always remembering that you are a Divine co-creator.

With your next breath, let all of your tension go and simply *be* for a moment or two, even longer if possible. Enjoy sitting and breathing deeply, empty of all thought, free of any agenda, centered in the moment. Feel this vibration of being connected to Source. Notice how peaceful, content, and even energized you feel. This,is the power of your Spirit, and it's available to you at all times. It is the real you. *Remember this.*

### Daily Ritual: Set Your Intention

Take a few moments each morning to set your intentions for the day. Ask yourself what you would like to accomplish. What is important to your Spirit? In what areas are you in need of guidance? In what ways would you like to receive support, ideas, and solutions? If possible, announce your intentions and requests out loud, ideally in prayer form.

Your own voice is one of the most powerful sounds in the Universe. As you say your intentions out loud in prayer, you can tell by the vibration behind them whether or not you are genuinely committed to creating these intentions. If you speak with conviction, your Spirit gets behind your intentions and seeks to assist you.

If you speak with hesitation, however, your Spirit refrains from helping you. This is because the Universe co-creates, following your creative lead. The Universe can and will meet you halfway. It will assist the process as long you ask for guidance and inspiration with pure intention, not as a victim but as a responsible co-creator.

As part of your practice of daily morning prayers, set your intentions and ask for assistance in every way possible. Then open your heart and mind to receive what you ask for in the form of intuition and inspiration. Follow this guidance without hesitation. This is flow in the highest order. Trust your intuitive vibes, and act on them!

### Coming Full Circle

One of the most life-affirming experiences we can have is that of being an instrument of service to others, especially when that opportunity is given to us by surprise. Love flowing to us is a gift from God to us, and the gift grows ever greater when we allow it to flow though us and onward without hesitation or fear. This is one of the highest forms of flow we can enter.

My daughter Sonia (she shares my name, as do I with my own mother in a long line of Sonias), and her best friend, Mary, were in the final weeks of college before graduating. They were under a great deal of pressure. Not only were final exams looming before them, and their senior theses yet to be written, but also the extended, emotional good-byes with their dearest friends were adding to their mental and physical overload. Furthermore, they were facing the question of what to do with their lives, which lurked conspicuously at the edges of their minds, burdening their already anxious state.

The job market was the worst it had been in more than 50 years, and the support they enjoyed from their parents as students was soon coming to an end as they stepped into the world. It seemed as if their carefree futures had suddenly contracted into a claustrophobic state of "not enough," and it was terrifying. There wasn't enough time to study, not enough time to say good-bye to friends, not enough inspiration and original ideas to finish their final papers, and not enough money or jobs to support them after their diplomas were placed in their hands. For Sonia and Mary, life seemed overwhelmingly difficult, leaving them both feeling paralyzed.

During one particularly stressful evening, the girls, in a spontaneously rebellious mood, decided to put aside their obligations and go out for drinks and a burger at one of their favorite outdoor cafés in Portland, where they lived. It wasn't really a sensible decision. Not only did they not have the time to indulge in an evening off from their work, but they also didn't have the money to go out and splurge. Rationalizing it all the way to the restaurant as a necessary time-out, they knew that such a choice would catch up with them tomorrow. Still, they were willing to deal with the consequences. My daughter later told me that it was something that they both just felt they needed to do, so they went with it.

No sooner had they sat down and ordered their drinks and meal when they noticed a scary-looking homeless man aimlessly wandering down the street. He was shouting angrily, causing most people to either look away uncomfortably or gaze directly at him in total disgust. He wasn't an unusual sight in Portland since there are a lot of lost men and women living on the streets there—many of them addicted to alcohol or methamphetamine. Yet as the disheveled man continued weaving back and forth, raging on, he seemed more menacing than most.

Sure enough, he caught Sonia's eye and beelined directly toward her. Mary groaned as he approached, mostly in fear, as he was clearly unstable and seemed eager to start a fight with anyone who would give him the slightest provocation. Sonia just took a breath and smiled at him.

"I'm hungry!" he yelled indignantly, as he walked right up to their table. "I'm a Vietnam veteran, and I fought for this country. Now I'm starving, and no one will even look me in the eye. I just want some food."

Sonia immediately felt compassion for him and calmly said, "I understand. That must be terrible. Please just calm down, and have a seat. I'll order you anything you want to eat."

Still uncertain of his mental state, she pointed toward a table a few feet away from theirs and said, "You can sit there and look this over," as she handed him a menu. "I'll get the waiter."

Surprised by her response, he hesitated and then stormed over to the table she had suggested and threw himself into a chair. He glanced at the menu and then flung it aside just as fast, obviously too distressed or unstable to even read it. Still seething, he defiantly looked right at her and commanded, "I want a cheeseburger, fries, and a chocolate milkshake." He stared angrily toward her as he made the request, as if daring her to refuse.

"No problem," Sonia responded. "I can get that for you. You just sit here. It will come, but it's going to take a few minutes."

By now the waiter recognized that Sonia was trying to help the man, and he joined in the goodwill. He jotted down the order as Sonia dictated, and brought the wretched man a place setting and glass of water. The homeless man refused to look the waiter in the eye. Sonia wondered if that was because he didn't want to risk seeing another look of disapproval coming toward him. If she were in his place, she realized that she would probably defiantly look away, too.

Once the waiter left, Sonia encouraged the man to relax, which he seemed to do for about 30 seconds. Then he was up again, pacing back and forth. Suddenly, he stopped in his tracks and looked as if he were seeing a ghost. Sonia, who had been watching him, followed his gaze. Walking down the street toward them was a well-dressed man carrying a briefcase. The homeless man walked right up to him and grabbed his arm forcefully. Sonia gasped, fearing that the unsuspecting gentleman was about to be attacked. Instead, he looked at the homeless man in shock, and then said, "Mark? Is that you, man? I don't believe it!"

The two men embraced and started crying. They were only a few feet away from Sonia's table, so she could hear their entire conversation.

The well-dressed man spoke again, "Oh my God, bro, I haven't seen you since 'Nam! What the hell *happened* to you?"

The homeless man shook his head. Suddenly sounding very meek and apologetic, he answered, "I didn't do so well after we returned. I had a really bad case of PTSD, and I haven't been able to get on my feet. It's been really hard."

The well-dressed man then grabbed the stinking, wretched, filthy man and gave him the warmest, most heartfelt hug she'd ever seen two men share. "I'm so sorry this happened to you. You're such a good guy. This is unbelievable. I can't stand to see you this way." He then took out his wallet and emptied it of all the cash, and shoved it into his old friend's hand. "Here, take this for now," he insisted. "And here's my card. Call me tomorrow, and I promise I'll help you get back on your feet."

They hugged once more for a really long time, and then the well-dressed guy said, "Call me! I mean it. Call me." Then he continued on his way, shaking his head, as if he couldn't believe what had just happened.

The homeless guy stood still for a moment and then put the money in his pocket. He turned around and walked right up to Sonia, and asked, "Do you believe in God?"

Stunned by the interaction that had just taken place and surprised by his question, she hesitated for a second, but then said, "Yes, I do."

"Do you believe in miracles?"

Still absorbing what she'd just witnessed, she answered once again, "Yes, I do."

"Well, you just caused a miracle to happen to me. If you hadn't ordered my food and asked me to sit down and wait for it, I never would have run into my friend. You just saved my life."

Just then his meal came out. The waiter served it to him as if he were one of the restaurant's most-valued customers and not the ranting lunatic he appeared to be only moments earlier.

Sonia returned to her own meal with Mary, both silent with eyes wide open and staring at each other.

The man wolfed down his food in seconds, then got up and approached their table once more.

"Thank you," he said. "Thank you so much." He turned and quietly walked away.

Sonia looked at Mary and said, "I guess that's why we had to stop what we were doing and come here for dinner. We had to help this guy out, and we didn't know it."

"You're absolutely right," Mary agreed. "Seeing what he's been dealing with, I guess we really have nothing to worry about, do we? We're so lucky not to suffer the way he does."

"That's true. We really are."

Still processing the strange unfolding of events, Sonia suddenly blurted out, as if speaking to her own uncertain future, "Things surprisingly work out, so why worry? And we have everything to do with the fact that they can and do work out if we're willing to help each other."

It was time to leave and the girls asked for their bill, and the waiter told them that there wasn't one. Their dinner, as well as the homeless man's, was on the house. He paid for them. The night was a gift all the way around.

## Tuning In

The final step in our transformation into Divine beings who live in blessed flow is that of empathy, of responding to life with compassion and a willingness to help other people every single day. As Divine beings, we instinctively recognize that we're all interconnected in such a sublime way that our egos alone can't fully grasp it. We are never really isolated or disconnected from others, except in our own minds, and as soon as we remember and act on that wisdom, all doors that appear closed, all avenues that seem shut off, suddenly open up.

We move in the highest form of flow when our hearts are the force that moves us. When we stop judging, overthinking, worrying, and separating ourselves from others and from God, and simply follow our natural design to love without hesitation or fear, life becomes a blessed symphony of miracles. As Mother Teresa, the great miracle worker of our time, and one of the most divinely transformed human beings to walk this earth, once said, "We cannot do great things. We can do only do little things with great love."

The choice to do little things with great love is the most fundamentally transforming of all. It is only this that ensures that our shift into Divine consciousness is complete. It is the final awareness we must embrace before we can experience the full power of our intuition, and the only information our egos need to learn and practice. To live each day filled with love for life and for our fellow humans, and to express our love through small and consistent acts of compassion, both toward ourselves and others, marks our truest graduation into a completely Divine state of being. The ego would like us to believe that it's far more difficult and complicated than this. It is not. Love is all there is to know, to live, and to share.

### Asking the Questions

Close your eyes and calmly breathe in and out through your nose. Start with a sigh or two to help you relax. Massage your jaw and throat a little to release even more tension and fear held in that part of your body, your expression center. Feel the energetic tension that your racing mind creates in your body. Do you notice how it drains your energy, your life force, your kefi, right out of you?

Now relax the tension in your neck and throat as much as possible with a few gentle stretches and take in a deep, easy, belly-filling breath. Don't force your breath to enter your body by raising your shoulders and holding your head back. Rather, keep your shoulders comfortably relaxed and down, and allow your belly to pull the air in naturally without any tension at all. Exhale by releasing the sound "Ah," and then bring the corners of your lips up to your ears in a gentle smile.

Next, take out your journal and turn your attention inward. Contemplate each of the following questions, and invite your Spirit, your most authentic Self, to respond to each one. Give yourself plenty of time to feel the genuine response coming from your heart, the source of your power.

- In what ways could you be more loving and compassionate toward yourself? Are you often critical of yourself? Do you consider yourself unworthy?

- In what ways do you judge others? By their looks? By their lack of accomplishments or status? Whether or not they are educated? By their seeming weaknesses or vulnerabilities? Are these the same things you judge and criticize in yourself?

- When you're around weak or vulnerable people, how do you generally behave? Are you inclined to offer your help or do you tend to look away?

- When it comes to intuition, do you follow your instincts and act, even when your rational mind fights you?

- Can you spontaneously allow yourself to depart from set plans and go with new influences or impulses, or do you stick to the plan and resist spontaneous diversions?

- Do you genuinely feel a spiritual connection between yourself and others? Does sharing with people you know or even strangers come easily to you?

- When was the last time you spontaneously experienced the flow of goodness toward you? How did it come about?

- When was the last time you expressed the flow of goodness toward another person? What were you doing? How did you feel afterward?

- How does being in the flow of compassionate love feel when it does occur? Familiar? Secure? Surprising? Tentative? Natural?

After writing down your answers, set aside your journal and remain seated. Close your eyes and calmly breathe in and out through your nose. Start with a sigh or two to help you relax. Recall a kindness you did for someone. Focus on the way you felt during and afterward. Hold on to the feeling of openness and unconditional love in your heart.

With your next breath, let all of your tension go and simply *be* for a moment or two, even longer if possible. Enjoy sitting and breathing deeply, empty of all thought, free of any agenda, centered in the moment. Feel this vibration of being connected to Source. Notice how peaceful, content, and even energized you feel. This is the power of your Spirit, and it's available to you at all times. It is the real you. *Remember this.*

### *Daily Ritual: Cultivate Compassion*

Be *compassionate.* The definition of the word is "a deep awareness of the suffering of another coupled with the wish to relieve it." This doesn't mean that you're supposed to come to the rescue of every troubled soul you meet. It simply invites you to treat those in need with dignity, kindness, patience, and generosity to the best of your ability. People in need cross your path so that you can practice living as a Divine, conscious being. The benefit of your loving-kindness is yours to keep. For all you know, those you help may be angels in disguise, eagerly assisting in advancing your education as a fully transformed spiritual being.

Graduate once and for all from the limitations of the ego and establish the deepest possible connection to your inner voice—your loving, powerful Spirit—by choosing to live compassionately every day.

✻

When you have setbacks, lose patience, judge, or criticize others, notice how unhappy you feel, how "unwhole" and isolated. Then forgive yourself and start over. Don't exclude yourself from the circle of love and compassion for all of life.

As you're journeying through the four steps of transformation, remember that you are an integral part of the circle. Breathe in compassion, breathe out compassion. Breathe in love, breathe out love. Breathe in as Spirit, breathe out as Spirit. Enjoy the benefits, and feel your own unlimited Divine power.

✻  ✻  ✻

# AFTERWORD

## The New Frontier

Moving through the four steps of transformation as we learn to listen to and be guided by the authentic power of our intuition is a dynamic and challenging process. Each step requires our full attention, evokes our worst fears, challenges our limited beliefs, and demands relentless courage, as we're asked to grow in ways that aren't always comfortable or easy.

As we leave the false security of the ego and move back into a true relationship with the Universe as Divine spiritual beings, we often feel as if we're stepping into the abyss and being led into oblivion. In letting go of the old ways of the ego, we die a little with each step we take toward our Spirit. This death—although a welcome liberation from the prison of our own making—can nonetheless be frightening.

Reaching the last step of transformation and falling into the flow of Divine Spirit is not an ending; rather, it's a wonderful new beginning. As soon as we surrender in love and compassion to the guidance of our Spirit, we find ourselves at the threshold of a deeper awakening, followed by a profound degree of discovery.

As we further surrender our carefully crafted identities, we experience even more magnificent experiences of flow.

The process of Divine expansion and the journey back to Spirit never ends. Not even with death. It just repeats at higher levels of consciousness, an endless spiral of increasing light as we grow brighter—vibrating at increasingly higher frequencies of consciousness and merging into the one power of pure Spirit, pure love.

The question "Will it ever end?" is one we'll never have an absolute answer to as long as we are in human form. We can only continue to transform our ego, tune in to our inner guidance, follow our light, and remember to live in the power of our Spirit through daily practice.

Trust that your choice to follow the guidance of your Spirit will be the best choice you can ever make. Know that you'll move away from any feelings of fear if you faithfully practice tuning in and following your heart. Little steps are all that any of us, as humans, can make. Yet each step—in the form of the simple daily practices shared throughout this book—will bring you closer to the great light of love, which is your Spirit.

The hour of transformation from limited fearful ego to empowered light being of Spirit is now. The Universe is demanding that we all evolve, for our light can no longer be trapped in the darkness of our fears. We're all destined to remember who we are, beautiful beings of light and love, and live as we are designed to be: as empowered, creative, joyful, confident, loving spiritual beings, filled with the dance of light, the laughter and play of our Spirit, and the endless love and compassion that is our true nature.

You are not alone—you never were. None of us is. You're supported at all times and in all ways by unseen holy forces of love that you cannot even begin to imagine. You are connected to all of humanity and to the heart of God. Although you may feel afraid, there is nothing to fear. You are safe. There is no enemy to fight, no struggle to undertake. There are only the dark and threatening walls of your own confusion to dismantle. Tune in to your intuition, and trust what you feel. Beyond these artificial barriers lie peace and the greatest of all power: the fearless ability to love.

Slowly and happily, all of humankind is learning to flow. Continue to reclaim the joy and power of your Spirit by maintaining a faithful practice of listening to your intuition. Devote yourself to it. Make tuning in to your authentic Self, which is love, the most important thing in your life, and your peaceful transformation will be ensured.

May you be blessed and loved, and may you live in the power of your Spirit forever.

As always, all my love,

*Sonia*

❋    ❋    ❋

# EMPOWERING RITUALS OF AN INTUITIVELY GUIDED BEING

On a beautiful piece of paper, such as parchment or your favorite stationery, write down the statements on the following page and place the sheet on your altar. Alternatively, you can simply photocopy the page. Every morning when you visit your altar, reach for this paper and read the statements out loud, slowly and clearly.

Sit silently and contemplate these intentions for a few moments. Acknowledge that by living them, you allow the power of your Spirit, your true Self, to lead your life. Focus your attention specifically on where your behavior isn't presently aligned with these intentions and resolve to change them one at a time.

Next, gently return the paper back to your altar. Reading these statements out loud on a regular basis will deeply imprint them into your subconscious mind, where they'll start to integrate as new patterns of behavior at the deepest level of your awareness. Soon you will memorize them and naturally begin to shape your life choices and responses around them. Eventually, you'll no longer need to think about making these Spirit-based choices; they'll come to you automatically. As the old saying goes, "If you name it, you claim it."

Claim your authentic Divine self with these intentions, and commit to allowing your Spirit to become the leader of your life each and every day from now on. The more you work on it, the more empowered and peaceful you will feel.

*As an empowered, intuitively guided being, I choose to . . .*

- Live for the moment.
- Be open to the guiding Spirit dwelling in me.
- Breathe in Spirit before I think, speak, or act.
- Acknowledge the Divine Spirit in all living beings.
- Consciously remember to breathe and tune in to my inner guidance every day.
- Actively become aware of and peel away my limiting ego patterns.
- Easily release what no longer serves a useful purpose in my life.
- Openly acknowledge my intuition each day.
- Make choices that are aligned with my authentic Self.
- Speak my heart's truth with love.
- Keep the fire of my Spirit burning.
- Do something I love every day.
- Surrender into the flow.
- Accept the ebb.
- Set my intentions, and follow my inspirations daily.
- Pray for guidance.
- Be compassionate toward all beings, including myself.
- Show gratitude for everything in life.
- Enjoy the gift of my life.
- Let my Spirit lead.

❄ ❄ ❄

# ABOUT THE AUTHOR

**Sonia Choquette** is a world-renowned author, storyteller, vibrational healer, and six-sensory spiritual teacher who is in international demand for her guidance, wisdom, and capacity to heal the soul. She is the author of several best-selling books, including the *New York Times* bestseller *The Answer Is Simple . . . Love Yourself, Live Your Spirit!; Ask Your Guides: Connecting to Your Divine Support System; Trust Your Vibes: Secret Tools for Six-Sensory Living;* and *Soul Lessons and Soul Purpose: A Channeled Guide to Why You Are Here*—plus numerous audio programs and card decks.

Sonia was educated at the University of Denver and the Sorbonne in Paris, and holds a Ph.D. in metaphysics from the American Institute of Holistic Theology. She resides with her family in Chicago.

Website: www.soniachoquette.com

❋    ❋    ❋

# Notes

# Notes

# Notes

# Notes

## Hay House Titles of Related Interest

*YOU CAN HEAL YOUR LIFE, the movie,*
starring Louise L. Hay & Friends
(available as a 1-DVD program and an expanded 2-DVD set)
Watch the trailer at: www.LouiseHayMovie.com

*THE SHIFT, the movie,*
starring Dr. Wayne W. Dyer
(available as a 1-DVD program and an expanded 2-DVD set)
Watch the trailer at: www.DyerMovie.com

❄

*BEING OF POWER: The 9 Practices to Ignite an Empowered Life,*
by Baron Baptiste

*LOVEABILITY: Knowing How to Love and Be Loved,*
by Robert Holden, Ph.D.

*101 WAYS TO JUMP-START YOUR INTUITION,* by John Holland

*POSITIVE VIBES: Inspiring Thoughts for Change & Transformation,*
by Gordon Smith

*WISHES FULFILLED: Mastering the Art of Manifesting,*
by Dr. Wayne W. Dyer

*YOU CAN CREATE AN EXCEPTIONAL LIFE,*
by Louise L. Hay and Cheryl Richardson

*YOU DO KNOW: Learning to Act On Intuition Instantly,*
by Becky Walsch

All of the above are available at your local bookstore,
or may be ordered by contacting Hay House (see next page).

❄

# Free e-newsletters from Hay House, the Ultimate Resource for Inspiration

Be the first to know about Hay House's dollar deals, free downloads, special offers, affirmation cards, giveaways, contests, and more!

Get exclusive excerpts from our latest releases and videos from *Hay House Present Moments*.

Enjoy uplifting personal stories, how-to articles, and healing advice, along with videos and empowering quotes, within *Heal Your Life*.

Have an inspirational story to tell and a passion for writing?  Sharpen your writing skills with insider tips from *Your Writing Life*.

## Sign Up Now!

*Get inspired, educate yourself, get a complimentary gift, and share the wisdom!*

**http://www.hayhouse.com/newsletters.php**

**Visit www.hayhouse.com to sign up today!**

HAY HOUSE

HAYHOUSE RADIO
*radio for your soul*

HealYourLife.com